Second Edition

Are You Sure
You're the
Principal?

For Evan Buford Villani, my son, and Adria Buford Villani, my daughter: I love you this much, "just because."

Second Edition ───────────

Are You Sure *You're the* *Principal?*

A Guide for New and Aspiring Leaders

Susan Villani

Foreword by
Roland S. Barth

CORWIN PRESS
A SAGE Company
Thousand Oaks, CA 91320

For information:

Corwin Press
A SAGE Company
2455 Teller Road
Thousand Oaks, California 91320
www.corwinpress.com

SAGE Ltd.
1 Oliver's Yard
55 City Road
London EC1Y 1SP
United Kingdom

SAGE Pvt. Ltd.
B 1/I 1 Mohan Cooperative
   Industrial Area
Mathura Road, New Delhi 110 044
India

SAGE Asia-Pacific Pte. Ltd.
33 Pekin Street #02-01
Far East Square
Singapore 048763

Printed in the United States of America.

Library of Congress Cataloging-in-Publication Data

Villani, Susan. Are you sure you're the principal?: A guide for new and aspiring leaders/Susan Villani. — 2nd ed.
      p. cm.
Includes bibliographical references and index.
ISBN 978-1-4129-5814-1 (cloth : acid-free paper)
ISBN 978-1-4129-5815-8 (pbk. : acid-free paper)
   1. School principals—United States. 2. Women school principals—United States. 3. Educational leadership—United States. I. Title.

LB2831.92.V55 2008
371.2'012—dc22   2008003608

This book is printed on acid-free paper.

08   09   10   11   12   10   9   8   7   6   5   4   3   2   1

Acquisitions Editor:	Debra Stollenwerk
Editorial Assistant:	Allison Scott
Production Editor:	Veronica Stapleton
Copy Editor:	Geof Garvey
Typesetter:	C&M Digitals (P) Ltd.
Proofreader:	Theresa Kay
Indexer:	Kirsten Kite
Cover Designer:	Monique Hahn

Contents

Foreword

The knowledge base for improving schools is thought to reside in large-scale social science research. When policymakers in Sacramento, Tallahassee, or Washington want to know what is right or wrong with public schools, what should be changed, and how school leaders should accomplish this, they turn to the work of a Richard Elmore or a Peter Senge.

There is another knowledge base of inestimable value for the improvement of public schools. This "literature" is much less evident than formal research in discussions about school reform. Craft knowledge is the massive collection of experiences and learning that those who live and work under the roof of the schoolhouse inevitably amass during their careers. These are the insights garnered by teachers, principals, guidance counselors, librarians, school secretaries, and parents about important matters such as parent involvement, staff development, curriculum development, discipline, teaching, leadership, and school improvement.

Tragically, the wisdom from the craft rarely is viewed—by outsiders or by school people themselves—as legitimate or rigorous, let alone useful, in the important work of school improvement. I believe there are three reasons why this happens: First, when a 4th-grade teacher or a principal speaks, it is believed that out will come, not craft knowledge, but a war story. "Let me tell you about the time I tried to fire a teacher." Eyes glaze over.

War stories are descriptions of practice, verbal portraits of the events of the schoolhouse. Craft knowledge is description of practice accompanied by analysis of practice. "Let me tell you about the time I tried to fire a teacher—and here's what I learned from it. If I were to do it again, here's how I would do it differently." Such hard-won learning from practice is the gold of the realm.

Second, in the cruel world of schools, which places practitioners in the position of competitor with others for scarce recognition and resources, few are willing to share their gold, panned from years of experience, lest their fellows come to occupy a position of greater respect and admiration.

Finally, even if a teacher or principal chooses to, it is often not safe for a practitioner to disclose his or her craft knowledge to fellow educators. It is likely to be greeted in a faculty room with put-downs: "Big deal. I've been doing that for years."

Thus, our profession seems to neither welcome nor value either the giving or the receiving of craft knowledge. What a tragic loss to the profession, to the professionals, and to the cause of school reform!

I recently completed and published a collection of stories about my many years sailing the coast of Maine. In the course of writing this book, I have come to learn something of the extraordinary power of storytelling and the gifts that it can bring to the teller and the audience alike. In addition, I am discovering that storytelling may provide an important key, capable of unlocking the wisdom of the educational, as well as the nautical, craft.

Susan Villani has discovered this key as well. She tells us that "we need to hear more stories about leadership." The book you are about to read is replete with stories and vignettes from her 21-year career as a public school principal. Embedded in them is a treasure trove of craft knowledge. Her learning on the job, courageously disclosed, becomes strikingly accessible, useful, and even healing for aspiring and practicing principals alike.

I think you will find this collection of stories, and the analysis that accompanies each, deeply personal, engaging, and introspective. Above all, you will find that through storytelling, Susan Villani brings an abundance of authenticity.

Enjoy, and make wise use of the gift of the hard-won wisdom offered by this accomplished and reflective practitioner.

Roland S. Barth
Founding Director
Harvard Principals' Center

Preface

THE LEADERSHIP CHALLENGE

Our schools need leaders who have vision and are prepared to act on it—leaders who continually promote growth and explore alternative approaches to learning, community building, problem solving, and teacher empowerment. When we find creative, talented, and visionary leaders, we want them to bring their knowledge, talent, and skills to every aspect of their principalship.

Sometimes, when leaders share more of themselves, people may feel confused and even threatened. Although leaders often are chosen because of their strengths, when they act authentically (consistently working from their beliefs and passions), the school community may critique and try to modify the very attributes that distinguished them.

In the United States, we may be facing a crisis of leadership in education. The U.S. Department of Labor projected that 40 percent of the country's 93,200 principals are nearing retirement. Sixty-six percent of respondents to a National Association of Elementary School Principals survey indicated that they will retire or be retired by 2012. School superintendents are saying that they are not getting the quantity or caliber of applicants they did in the past. Many new principals have less teaching and administrative experience than their predecessors. Now more than ever, new principals need mentoring and coaching from their experienced colleagues.

This book serves to encourage and support leaders in being authentic and reflecting on their practice and to educate school communities about effective leadership. It is important for staff, teachers, administrators, families, and the larger community to understand that to be effective, leaders must lead in their own ways—and that the resulting changes in the schools are in the service of promoting an even better education for all students. When people understand this, they will be more inclined to work through their differences, pooling talents and resources in the spirit of working together.

MENTORING THROUGH STORIES FOR ASPIRING, EXPERIENCED, AND REFLECTIVE PRINCIPALS

I wrote *Are You Sure You're the Principal? A Guide for New and Aspiring Leaders* to share craft wisdom in a personal way, through stories and commentary. Stories make ideas about leadership easily accessible to readers interested in the practical as well as the theoretical. Readers tell me that they identify with the situations described in the book. *Are You Sure You're the Principal?* chronicles my path in leadership, from the excruciating challenges of my first year as a principal through my career as an effective and respected leader, a trainer of leaders, and a leader of a leadership organization.

This book illustrates leadership that is authentic and reflective. I share my insights about intention, communication, conflict, and building community to provide opportunities for readers to do self-reflection as well as to discuss their beliefs and practice. Study guides at the end of the book include quotes about leadership from 15 leaders, activists, and writers and offer questions to ponder or discuss that refer to the entire book and each individual chapter. These study guides are designed for individual readers, aspiring and experienced principals who are studying educational administration and leadership, and study groups of practitioners.

Readers tell me that my self-reflection has inspired them to explore past and present leadership experiences. Understanding these influences on their current practice helps aspiring, new, and experienced principals enhance their effectiveness and job satisfaction.

I wish there had been a book like this when I first became a principal—a book in which an experienced leader shared her or his craft wisdom in a personal way, through stories. I hope that you'll find that reading my book is like sitting with an experienced colleague and hearing some ways that she makes sense of her practice.

Two organizing principles structure this book. Core issues of leadership are named in chapter titles and illustrated and discussed through stories; the evolution of a leader is also portrayed. Commentary, artwork, dialogue, correspondence, and other writings punctuate the stories.

FOR THOSE INTERESTED IN SCHOOL LEADERSHIP AND REFLECTIVE PRACTICE

Aspiring administrators need to think about a variety of ways of leading in order to discover what is congruent with their values and educational philosophy. Initially, they may be most concerned about the challenges facing principals and candid reflections of an experienced principal. Practicing administrators and school leaders identify with the issues presented in this book. Principals have said that they resonated with the feelings that were described. Anyone interested in the experience of someone atypical of the role at the time of her experience, or a relational approach to leadership, may find these stories engaging, whether the reflections affirm, inform, or provoke the reader's thinking. There are many more books about educational leadership written by men than by women, so both men and women may be interested in a woman's reflection on her career and growth. Parents are often curious about the schools their children attend and welcome more insight into school management and leadership. Teachers who wish to expand the lens through which they view their own school leaders may find insight in reading about another principal's reflection on practice. Leaders in other fields, such as business, may benefit from this book; seeing leadership in another context provides a way to clarify and expand their concept of leadership. In addition, these stories offer a powerful invitation for all readers to reflect on leadership and the importance of being authentic.

What's New in This Second Edition

Chapters have been rewritten and in some cases reorganized and retitled. Study guides for each chapter and a study guide for all chapters have been added. A concluding chapter is also new to this edition.

I hope that this edition prompts people to discuss leadership with others in courses, study groups, books groups, and colleague-to-colleague. Sharing and reflecting on each other's experiences and beliefs about leadership can be enormously challenging and affirming. Discussing and possibly disagreeing with something written or shared in conversation can be a powerful form of professional development. Promoting reflection to enhance practice is the work I most enjoy doing now, through either mentoring, coaching, teaching, or writing. I wrote this book to serve people interested in such reflection and hope that you find it does.

OVERVIEW OF THE CHAPTERS

Chapter 1: Are You Sure You're the Principal?

I have never believed in stereotypes. I have fought against them my whole life. But if you had asked me when I first became a principal to describe a leader, a stereotypical character would have emerged. It would have been someone who acted and influenced, someone who commanded respect. It would have been a prominent presence whose opinions were known, a person who could handle any situation.

This first chapter is about coming to terms with stereotypes and distortions, beginning with my own. These stories are about learning that regardless of what I presented, people's expectations of me may have altered their perceptions. My early experiences as a principal confirmed that becoming the educational leader of a school involves a lot more than simply being appointed to the position.

Chapter 2: Working Through Conflict

The stories in this chapter are about conflict, communication, and the effect of power on both. Even though I could teach students ways to resolve conflicts with their peers, I found it much more difficult to identify, understand, and work through the conflicts I was having with staff members. Here issues of roles and power were constantly present. Some of our interactions were excruciating. My efforts to be authentic were not always understood or welcomed. Conflict, isolation, and group dynamics have, at times, undermined, but also strengthened, my resolve to be part of and lead a school community I respected and to earn the respect of its members.

Chapter 3: Communicating
Who We Are and What We Believe

I reflect on ways that I concealed or revealed my feelings and thoughts during various times in my career and why I had developed these behaviors. I consider how to be more forthcoming in the interest of clarity and because I intuitively knew that authentic leadership required the ability to express outrage or tell truths.

Chapter 4: Building Community

We all need recognition and acceptance. The stories in this chapter reflect what I have done as a leader to help others learn about self-acceptance and acceptance of others. While hiring new staff to the school community and promoting teacher development through self-reflection, I focused on trust building and the necessity of finding common ground.

Over time, I moved from trying to fix things alone to facilitating joint problem solving and group decision making. By reflecting on how my disposition and action affected the outcomes, I learned that empowerment and innovation require leadership that inspires and is built on a foundation of trust.

Chapter 5: Advisers, Mentors, and Allies

The stories in this chapter are about guidance, support, and affirmation. Being reminded of our traits and abilities can keep us from getting bogged down by confusion and self-doubt in challenging times. For beginners, mentors are invaluable teachers and supporters. But even experienced leaders need to be validated, to seek support, and to recognize and accept it when it is offered. The fulfillment that comes to those who mentor is often one of the most rewarding aspects of their careers. Taking the next steps in our evolution as leaders and encouraging others to do the same is how we can nourish and sustain leadership that is authentic.

Chapter 6: Reflecting on a Career:
Committing to Pursue Professional Passion

Principals may at times reconsider their commitment to the role or think about being a principal elsewhere. They may also be enticed to consider other roles in education. This chapter seeks to raise issues of career fulfillment and things to consider when reflecting on goals, preferences, and opportunities. Some principals may be best served by making changes in their work and others by recommitting to being a principal.

Study Guides

A study guide for use with all chapters and study guides related to each chapter are included at the end of the book. They provide information from educational researchers and writers that are connected with key ideas in the book. These guides may be used for self-reflection, for group discussion or analysis, and for extending understanding of what it means to be a principal.

ACKNOWLEDGMENTS

With deep affection I acknowledge my father, Jerry Villani, and the memory of my grandmother, Catherine Villani, for their ongoing love, support, and belief in me. My father's confidence in me, urging me to keep learning and reaching further, helped me to achieve what sometimes seemed impossible. Another's confidence is, I believe, the best form of empowerment. I thank Greta Morrine, my teacher at age 10, who made us write a story every day. At the time I panicked, but my mother sat with me and advised me to "write it just as you would say it." For such good advice, and many tearful writing sessions at the kitchen table, I fondly remember my mother, Helen Hartzman Villani. In addition, I thank Mr. Burns, who signaled to me that my writing was worth sharing with more people when he chose my essay for the high school yearbook.

I benefited tremendously from Sharon Lowenstein's undivided attention and guidance as I began writing stories about my work. Laura Kranis was my writing coach as I wrote more stories, made a proposal to book publishers, and then created this book. Laura's thought-provoking questions led me to deeper understandings about my experiences and myself, and through her coaching I was able to improve my writing.

Receiving a phone call from Gracia Alkema, then the president of Corwin Press, two weeks after I sent her a book proposal was a totally unexpected and warm welcome to publishing. Robb

Clouse, the acquisitions editor who led me through the process of publishing the first edition of this book, has been thoughtful about my work and most kind. I am thankful for their nurturing and encouragement. I deeply appreciate Lizzie Brenkus's and Robb Clouse's support to do a second edition of this book. Deb Stollenwerk's advice and advocacy as the editor of this second edition have been particularly valuable because she understood my intent and writing very soon after she joined the project. Veronica Stapleton made the final stages of copyediting and proofs checking a painless process, for which I am ever grateful. Douglas Rife, Corwin's former president, conveyed caring and respect each time we met and affirmed my pleasure in being a Corwin author.

The physical process of writing can be a strain on one's body. I thank Mark Dynan, Mary Benkert, and Tony Phillips for care and suggestions through those challenges.

My deeply felt gratitude goes to Nancy Bronson, Marlyn Miller, and Susan Zellman-Rohrer for their nurturing support and assistance on the first edition I wrote, and Dan Conley, Rose Feinberg, and Kathleen Sciarappa for their review of my second edition manuscript and practical suggestions about ways to enhance the value of the study guides. Henry Damon, my husband, has shown his support in many ways, including running 100 feet of electrical cord so I could write outdoors, making more than his share of suppers, helping me to clarify my thinking about leadership, and reading the resulting revised manuscripts. Special thanks to Kathleen Sciarappa, Rose Feinberg, and Adam Tanney for sharing well-chosen resources I used in the study guides. My NECEL buddies have offered almost 30 years of wisdom, wit, and camaraderie. For long-term support and encouragement, my appreciation to Gwen Brooks, Cindy Dubea, Carol Harrington, Vickie Hornus, Jo Kelleher, Helen Regan, and Susan Stevenson. What I learned by the examples of two NECEL colleagues who became the dearest of friends and passed on prematurely, Marlyn Miller and Betty Allen, continue to influence me in profound ways.

I cherish the response George Graham, the superintendent who took a chance on me for my first principalship, spontaneously made: "Sometimes getting a grievance means you are doing something right." Roland Barth's warm endorsement of my work, in both this book and one I later wrote on mentoring and induction programs for new principals, underscores the work of his career-supporting principals.

I've acknowledged some of the people who influenced me and supported my writing, and the people who directly helped me make this book be my very best. How do I express my appreciation for the impact of so many others throughout my life? To my family, friends, colleagues, instructors, students, and their families who have taught, guided, challenged, mentored, taken a chance on, helped, accepted, valued, and encouraged me—to all of them, my heartfelt appreciation.

Susan Villani

Corwin Press would like to thank the following individuals for their contributions to the work:

Randel Beaver
Superintendent
Archer City ISD
Archer City, TX

Stephen Hegner
Principal
Brady Middle School
Pepper Pike, OH

Patrick J. Bingham
Director of Human
    Resources
Petersburg City Public
    Schools
Petersburg, VA

Ann Porter
Retired Elementary
    Principal
Grand Forks Public
    Schools
Grand Forks, ND

Steve Gruenert
Professor
Indiana State University
Terre Haute, IN

Dana Salles Trevethan
Principal
Turlock High School
Turlock, CA

About the Author

 Susan Villani knows about being a principal because she was one for 21 years. She has been the principal of schools with K–5, K–6, and 5–6 grade-level configurations, in three school districts, in two states. She was named Rhode Island's Young Career Woman of the Year by the Business and Professional Women's Association during her first year as a principal.

Not long after, Villani was elected president of the NorthEast Coalition of Educational Leaders (NECEL) and served on the board of directors for six years. She has taught graduate classes, spoken at conferences and meetings nationwide on leadership issues, coached aspiring administrators, and directed a resume assessment service. Her doctoral dissertation was on mentoring, and she has consulted with school systems and states to establish mentoring programs for new teachers.

Villani was commissioned by the Rhode Island Department of Education to write about programs on cultural awareness and career exploration that she co-developed, and she chaired the writing of the position paper of the Massachusetts Elementary School Principals' Association on prejudice and stereotyping. Her articles on mentoring have appeared in numerous publications, including the Principals' Center at Harvard, the University of Massachusetts, the Massachusetts Association of School Principals, and the American Association of School Personnel Officers. Villani wrote "A Principal Defined" in *Out of Women's Experience*, by Helen Regan and Gwen Brooks (1995, Corwin Press).

Villani has written *Mentoring Programs to Support New Teachers: Models of Induction and Support* and *Mentoring and Induction Programs That Support New Principals*. In addition, she has co-authored with Kathy Dunne *Mentoring New Teachers Through Collaborative Coaching: Linking Teacher and Student Learning* and an accompanying facilitator training guide.

Villani is currently a senior program/research associate at Learning Innovations at WestEd. She specializes in mentoring and coaching new teachers and new principals and teaching others to be coaches who promote reflection to improve practice. Villani has helped school districts and state departments of education develop and sustain mentoring, induction, and coaching programs that support new and experienced teachers. In addition, she has worked with school districts to develop collaborative school cultures.

Villani takes inspiration from the turtle: You have to stick your neck out to move forward.

Introduction

This book chronicles how I became a leader, and more important, an authentic leader. As I was coming of age in the 1960s, authority was being challenged on many fronts. So when people of my generation were in a position to lead, we were determined not to assert power over people. As teachers, we experimented with "open classrooms," putting much more emphasis on process than on curriculum. As parents, we had a very difficult time saying no, and we wouldn't have dreamed of saying, "Do it because I said so."

In an effort not to be bureaucratic or part of "the establishment," some of us tried nondirective leadership, in which there was validation of just about any point of view and little direction or guidance. To show our respect for people's autonomy, we resisted exercising authority, not realizing that acting on our own authority actually would be the most respectful course of action. When I became a principal in the late 1970s, I carried some of these ideas about leadership and authority with me.

I first arrived at my school in the summer, and the rooms were very dirty. The superintendent sent over a high school student to clean. I tentatively told the student what I wanted him to do, but phrased my direction more like a question. In fact, I ended every request with, "Is that all right?" At one point he shrugged his shoulders and looked away, and it dawned on me that he didn't want to be part of the decision-making process for each little thing I told him to do. He was uncomfortable being directed by someone who was so uncomfortable directing.

Throughout that fall, the students and the staff weren't at all sure what to make of a principal who smiled a lot and who sought more to help them resolve their conflicts than to punish them. In some ways, I was just as confused as they were. I had been a first-grade teacher and I began my principalship expecting to be a colleague with the teachers—more of a peer, but with different responsibilities.

The staff's reaction to me and to my way of leading was largely negative, and my newness contributed to my own uncertainty. I began to believe I would need traits other than the ones I had, in addition to all the competencies I needed to master as a principal. To veil my uncertainty, I thought I needed to present myself as having an assurance that I frankly didn't yet have. I thought I needed to act "as if" until I got there. I sought to become a principal they would respect and value, yet I wasn't sure how to do this. I mistakenly had confused being nonauthoritarian with being authentic, but authenticity does not mean abdicating authority. In addition, being authentic was even more of a challenge when so many people had their own, different expectations about what I should do and be.

I knew who I was as a person, but I needed to learn what it meant to be authentic as a principal. It would not work to define my leadership by the traits other people had used to define their leadership. I would be an authentic leader only if I used the attributes I already had to become the principal I aspired to be. With the help of mentors and other allies, I found the support I needed to once again feel and display the self-confidence I had had before becoming a principal. I was moving closer to true authenticity as a leader, which required claiming the authority of my own experience, claiming my own thoughts and feelings, and sharing them.

In my stories, I describe some of the most painful moments in my career, as well as some of the accomplishments of which I am most proud. I tell what happened, how I felt, and, sometimes, what sense I have made of it all.

My insights are filtered through my frame of reference, which includes being white and middle-class, with all the accompanying advantages of being in the majority. Still, as a young, female administrator, I had a profound, though temporary, experience of being the target of prejudice and stereotyping. I gained firsthand knowledge of what it feels like to be a minority. People who have been in the minority for any reason may have experienced some of the same things I did. As painful as those experiences were, they opened my eyes, and my passionate commitment to challenging all forms of prejudice was intensified as a result.

Some readers might assume that most women share my opinions, because leaders who have minority status in a specific context are sometimes perceived as representatives of their gender, race, or religion. This perception sometimes prevents people from saying what they think, not wanting to bear the responsibility of being spokespersons. I don't purport to represent others' experiences; I share my reflections in the hopes that they may be useful.

I am told that my experiences and perceptions have resonated with male and female administrators at different stages of their careers. While some issues have at times been the result of my gender, much of what I discuss comes with the territory of the principalship.

I have written these stories with care, wanting to tell them accurately and fairly. Yet I know that other people who were involved may remember and understand them differently. In an effort to be respectful of these differences, I have chosen not to name the people in my stories, except when given permission to credit writing, music, or artwork, because I want to be sensitive to people's feelings about how they are portrayed, even as I articulate my own "truths."

We may all benefit from the knowledge that others have had similar experiences and from hearing how they have dealt with their feelings and resolved their questions and dilemmas. I wish we could sit with a cup of tea and discuss our careers—our aspirations, feelings, and reflections. Because we can't do that, I share these stories as the closest approximation of a conversation that I can offer without being together.

We need to hear more stories about leadership—more voices—from people with diverse life experiences and perspectives. In our own ways, we lead and respond to people and situations. The different choices we make as leaders can inform the practices of all of us. My hope is that this book will engage you in thinking about your beliefs about leadership and about how you act on them. Please join me in thinking about leadership that is effective, visionary, and authentic.

This is not an important business letter so don't worry. . . . I appreciate the way you treat people, kind and caring. And the way everyone's equal. If it weren't for you I don't want to know what this school would be like. You know, it's a stereotype that all principals are mean and that they're all boys. You're definitely a stereotype-buster!

(Letter from Ali McGuirk, age 8,
after a conversation
in her class about stereotypes)

I'M FINALLY A PRINCIPAL

Ron Ferguson

I was once a classroom teacher.
Now I try to run a school.
When I first got the promotion
I thought it was really cool.

I knew it would be a challenge,
But I thought I was prepared,
So I stepped into the job
And started pulling out my hair!!!

Some teachers here expected me
To carry all their burdens
When I gave their burdens back
I was a quite unwelcome person.

And some parents thought they
    had the right
To pick their children's teachers.
When they didn't get their way
They said I was an *evil* creature.

But I never raised my voice
And always tried to be respectful
Even when I was contending
With adults who were neglectful.

No, instead I tried to model
What I hope will be the norm
When the teachers and the parents
Finally help this school reform.

If we're going to be successful
We have got to have a vision
Wherein grown-ups join together
In a shared and sacred mission.

Anyone who can't accept it
Is quite free to move along

And together we'll rejoice
When those who've held us back
    are gone.

For the future is upon us
And there is no time to waste
As new first graders
    learn to read
And soil their hands with paste.

When we blink they'll be in high
    school.
There is work to do each year
And we'll show the same
    commitment
To each child whom comes
    through here.

We are here to nurture children
In the best way that we can.
Anyone who shares this purpose
I invite to take my hand.

But I will not compromise
With those who choose
    the status quo.
I say, "One way or the other,
They have got to change, or go."

Yes sometimes it will be stressful
But you'll see that in the end
This will be a school we're proud of
THEN we all can be great friends.

I was once a classroom teacher.
Now I try to run a school.
Yes, it makes me pull my hair out.
Still, I think it's pretty cool.

Source: Used with permission from Ron Ferguson.

CHAPTER ONE

Are You Sure You're the Principal?

One time, in search of the principal, a visitor came to the front office. First he looked at the office clerk and asked if he was the principal. When the clerk, a man my age, indicated that he was not, the visitor turned to the secretary. Upon learning that she, a woman older than I, was not the principal, the person at last looked at me. He asked, "Where is the principal?"

FIRST IMPRESSIONS

"Carl, if you don't get your black butt in that building, I'm going to pick you up and carry you in there!" said Eva, the social worker, to a student in front of the school.

"Well, I'm not going," he replied angrily.

Her statement raised all kinds of red flags for me. My mind raced with questions: She's also African American. I'm not. Am I missing something? What did she mean? Why did she say it that way? How did Carl hear it? Unsure, I focused on the power struggle that was definitely unfolding in front of me.

It was the first day of school. I couldn't believe this was happening. Eva's threat to carry Carl inside might have seemed plausible if he had been 5 years old, but Carl was 11 years old and he looked very strong. At this point, my youth and my wish to be taken seriously as a new principal overrode my common sense. I was afraid that my authority was going to be judged by whether I assumed responsibility for Eva's threat, so I took over. When I looked at Eva, I was sure that she didn't expect me to insinuate myself into their conversation. I felt that I was being judged as someone who was too young, too inexperienced, or too scared to death to deal as effectively with this situation as she had.

Carl glared at me, as if to frighten me away, and he will never know how close I came to retreating. I took a deep breath and asked Carl why he didn't want to come into the school, trying to find a peaceful solution to this problem. He wouldn't talk with me and remained adamant that he was not entering. Finally, under what felt to me like Eva's watchful and challenging eyes, I honored her threat and told Carl that if he didn't go into the school by the time I counted to three, I would carry him in.

Carl was just half a foot shorter than I, and he was much more agile and strong. Yet I picked him up and struggled to get him up the four steps of the entrance and into the school. I think my initial success was because he was so stunned that I actually would pick him up that he didn't completely resist. By the time we were in the building and Carl saw that I was serious, he intensified his refusal.

There were eight more steps to get to the corridor, unfortunately complete with a long banister, which Carl grabbed to keep me from moving us forward. I reached for his fingers, trying to pry them off the banister while still trying to move his mass and mine up the stairs. For a few moments, it was not at all clear who would win this battle, and I was compelled by the feeling that my whole principalship was riding on my victory. That is probably how I was able to do the impossible: I got Carl up the stairs!

Huffing and puffing, I asked the office clerk to please call Carl's mother. The office clerk, a male, asked if I would like to call her while he held Carl, but after coming this far, there was no way I would let go.

Probably only a matter of minutes elapsed before Carl's mother arrived, but it seemed like an eternity to me. As soon as she looked at me, I started to explain why I was holding Carl with such force, fearful that she might be angry with me for doing so. To my surprise, she had in mind a much more vigorous handling of Carl than I ever would have considered. She glared at Carl and demanded to know why he had acted this way, forcing the principal to carry him in. I thought I detected some respect for my accomplishment in her voice as she interrogated him. Carl cowered in her presence and mumbled an apology to me before promising to be good and go to class. Carl's mother then directed her attention to me, saying that if I had any more trouble with Carl, I should just come and get her, and she would take care of him. It turned out that Carl's family resided across the street from the school and I mused how much simpler it would have been to go and speak to Carl's mother before embarking on my unheroic efforts.

After she left, I had a chance to notice what everyone else in the front office was doing. Everything had come to a standstill as people watched this drama unfold. I wonder whether they would have been as surprised if a large male principal had done what I did. They seemed very aware of what I had managed to do, and were perhaps a little frightened, not knowing how out of character this was for me.

As I stood there, I smoothed my clothing and ran my fingers through my hair in an attempt to achieve a look of composure. I felt something very strange happening to my lips. I went to a mirror and saw my lips swelling and turning a bluish purple before my eyes. Evidently I had bitten down on my lips in an effort to haul Carl up the stairs, and now I was wearing a badge of my courage in the form of bruised and swelling lips. Here I was, on the first day of school, and I looked like I had been in a brawl. Things were not starting out as I had envisioned, and this would be only the beginning of that problem for me.

LARGER THAN LIFE

I often wondered whether I would ever be widely regarded as the rightful inhabitant of my position. Despite my efforts to establish myself as a caring and collaborative principal, I was continually amazed at how my staff clung to their old expectations of a principal. In the minds of some people, the image of a principal is firmly rooted in stereotypes of age, gender, and style. Because I didn't match some teachers' expectations, they perceived my actions with a more skeptical eye. Whatever I did or said always seemed colored by people's projections.

The staff never guessed that loneliness and fear were two of my most frequent companions. I had taken a big risk to become a principal, leaving a school where I was well established as a 1st-grade teacher, and moving to another state where I didn't know a soul. Rumor had it that I lived with a celebrity, but no one knew who he was because "he traveled incognito!" I was flabbergasted. Another version of the rumor was that I lived with an international airline pilot, but he was often away, so that's why no one saw him. How I wished that either of those rumors were true, when in reality I lived alone and longed for companionship.

Where did those rumors come from? Certainly I didn't create this image, yet people seemed convinced it was true. The belief that I had a glamorous lifestyle with exciting men was some sort of exaggerated fantasy that was flattering and baffling. As I tried to understand what engendered these assumptions, I wondered whether their speculations were really about me at all or whether they were about their projections. If only people knew how solitary my after-school time was.

Around that same time, I decided to take up jogging for exercise and to reduce stress. At first, I could barely go around the block without being totally winded, but I persisted, jogging each morning with a couple of neighbors before showering and going to work. In a meeting one day, I reached for a doughnut and one of the teachers exclaimed, "You eat doughnuts?" She asked how I managed to jog eight miles a day if I ate junk food.

"Eight miles a day!" I exclaimed. "I am working my way up to an eighth of a mile a day. Where did you ever get the idea that I could jog so far?" She didn't know, but she had great difficulty believing me when I said it was not true. In our school, I think that some of the female teachers were not only comparing me with my predecessors, they also were measuring their lives against the exaggerated versions of the life they thought I had.

Children also have had specific ideas about my image and role. Years after I became a principal, a kindergartner noticed a refrigerator in the staff room and asked her teacher, "Is that what Dr. Villani does, buy food for everybody?" Fourteen years older and I had moved from jet-setter and athlete to mega-mother. Another teacher once told me that she had explained to her class that Dr. Martin Luther King Jr. was not a medical doctor, he was a doctor of freedom. "Oh, like Dr. Villani," replied an 8-year-old, elevating me to the stature of one of my own heroes.

One commonality of these stories is that they represent me as being larger than life. The principalship is a job that certainly has many responsibilities with many constituencies. Students, faculty, staff, families, and the community all have needs and expectations that often find their way to the principal's door. Maybe it shouldn't be surprising that there are stories depicting the principal as superhuman. It would seem to take someone with extraordinary abilities to do such a job successfully. Some people occasionally might revel in the myth of being perceived as superhuman, but I was very uncomfortable with it because it meant that I wasn't being seen as a real person. No one is superhuman, and any such expectation may result in disappointment, resentment, or anger.

During my first year, I found that some staff members were continually dissatisfied with much of what I was doing. I had difficulty pinpointing exactly why they were dissatisfied. I later realized their dissatisfaction was as much about the person I was and what I represented as about what I did. Although they were upset with their new principal, I believe they were even more upset that she could never be like her predecessors, let alone be superhuman. I was an unconventional principal in many ways, and it was very clear that some members of the staff were having great difficulty accepting me as their principal. Apparently, so did some of the community.

THE LOOK OF LEADERSHIP

Before I began my first principalship, I heard that a large crowd had stormed a school committee meeting to protest my appointment the previous month. One man summed up their upset this way: "There are three reasons why she shouldn't be principal. First, she's a 1st-grade teacher and this is a school for 5th and 6th graders; second, she's five-foot-four and weighs 117 pounds; and third, she's a girl!" According to this speaker, only males, preferably large ones, could be effective principals.

I was probably the youngest adult on the school staff and I was nervous. I was eager to show everyone that I was the right choice for the job, so I tried to look the part for a job that didn't typically include young women. Instead of the more colorful suit I wore for the interview, I chose more somber-looking suits to wear to work. Although I understand my reasoning, I feel sorry for the young woman I was who felt she had to look more like a man. Instead of being excited about beginning my new career as a principal, I chose to deny parts of myself in an effort to be accepted. I was being unauthentic in order to survive and to dispel the predictions of my failure based on the stereotypes held by some members of the community. While being female is not as unusual now, there are other aspects of difference that these days may engender similar feelings in a principal.

Early my first morning on the job, I met a man who had once been the school principal and was still an administrator in the system. He offered to help me place incoming students.

Walking over to the telephone that had once been his, he dialed the other principal. "Hello, Mike, this is Sam. I'm in the new little girl's office." I barely heard the rest, being so stunned by both the comment he had made and the fact that he didn't seem to have the slightest idea of how dismissed and invalidated it would make me feel—or did he?

While we waited for Mike to arrive, Sam reflected on his years as principal. He was a tall, muscular man, a former athlete who struck an imposing stance. "Some of the kids here are very tough," he told me. "I used to play a little basketball with them, one on one, you know. And somehow after we played, they got the message and they would straighten out." He looked me over, noting my size, and then added, almost with a note of concern, "I don't know what you're going to do." Neither did I.

A staff member once said, "When Sam was here, it was different. He was like a father to us." I was stung by those words. I remember how my head throbbed. I could never be the father for whom some longed, and I knew I didn't want to be a mother to them either. I couldn't possibly give them what they wanted and still be myself, but could we find a way for them to get enough of what they wanted, while I would retain enough of the person I was?

I remember the queasy feeling I had in my stomach when I heard Sam's words. He had described a school where physical intimidation was part of the climate, and it scared me. I even wondered, briefly, whether I should register for a karate class. In retrospect, it may have been Sam's comments that influenced my decision to respond to Carl as I did on the first day of school.

When I was a junior high school student, I had sympathized with boys who struggled because of the expectation that they show their strength by fighting. I had been glad to be a girl. Now, many years older, I was again facing expectations about using physical aggression to prove strength.

I didn't want to deal with discipline in Sam's way, not because I am a woman, but because it wasn't consistent with my values. I knew I couldn't lead in Sam's way, nor did I want to. I didn't know what my way would be, but I had to find a way that used my own strengths, the strengths I hoped I had.

The staff was confused by my attempts to lead; my approach was new to them. I was confused also; I had expected to be a principal the same way I had been a 1st-grade teacher, that is, to be authentic, to be myself. Yet it seemed that people had great difficulty accepting me the way I was. To Sam I was "the new little girl." To some teachers I was "larger than life." The more they saw what they expected, the harder I worked to be seen and understood as myself.

Sometimes I felt as though I was in one of those carnival mirrors in which the image was so distorted that I just wasn't me anymore. But we weren't in a carnival. This was real life, in a public school, with children to teach and a community to serve. They needed a real-life principal, not a distorted image of one.

So I became more and more intent on being a leader who was authentic and down-to-earth. Yet to overcome the varied and exaggerated perceptions, I had to put myself even more on display than I typically would in order to correct the misperceptions of the people in our school. People who are atypical for their role in a specific community may find that their differences are hard for others to understand and accept. If misperceptions result, we each must find our own way to be ourselves, while clarifying the misunderstandings.

I had not intended to be a leader who was so much in the center of things. I had wanted to work alongside colleagues and constituents as part of my leadership. I kept trying to change the focus from supposition about me to the educational goals and challenges of our school. I hoped, at least, that my persistence, as a demonstration of my caring, would convince more of the staff members to join me in doing what was best for the students. As things turned out, changing the focus from me to the needs of our school community was something I would have to do in each of my principalships.

A LITTLE RESPECT

Although I had 10 successful years in two principalships behind me, this, my third principalship, challenged me as painfully as when I began my first. When I began my career, I naively expected that if I worked very hard to do the right thing, people would respect me. I was confronted quickly with the reality that effort and good intentions are not enough to do the impossible, which is to please everyone. Although the specifics were different in this principalship, some of the underlying tensions were just as powerful and painful. In fact, they may have been worse. Because I had had 10 years of experience as a principal, I felt ashamed to be in this predicament at this point in my career. Colleagues at my previous school were openly distressed about my departure, yet some of the staff at my new school were up in arms about my arrival. I asked myself, "How could this be happening again?" Dashed expectations and unmet needs are powerful forces in the dynamics of schools at any time. Is it even more dramatic when the person in the role who is not meeting these needs is different from the predecessor, or possibly different from people's expectations?

In this school, some teachers and I had worked very hard to build bridges. To create a more positive school community, a "lip sync" show was planned, and students, families, and staff were invited to participate. I had chosen Aretha Franklin's well-known song, "Respect," for my performance, and several students joined me as backup singers and dancers. The night of the Lip Sync Show, I arrived wearing a gold lamé blouse, a tight black skirt, mesh stockings, and lots of makeup. I started to relax when a 5th-grade girl looked me up and down and said, "Gee, Dr. Villani, you should look like this all the time!" A male teacher whom I had hired the previous year was visibly surprised to see me like this and said with some disbelief, "Wow, Susan, you look . . . you look sexy!"

Once on stage, I dramatically asserted the song's chorus and its plea for a little respect. I danced freely to the music, to enhance this plea for respect. I had taken a risk by stating my needs, and what I believed to be the needs of the school community, on stage.

At first, the audience was so stunned they were silent, but soon enough they were laughing and whistling. By using humor and music, and portraying a character people could relate to, I had acknowledged a tense situation at school without seeming to be self-pitying or belligerent. By the end of the song, I felt that I had earned some of the respect I so badly needed if I was ever going to be effective in this principalship.

Respect is the cornerstone of mutual relationships. My vision of a school community where collaboration results in heightened understanding and achievement required that all members respect each other. The strong differences of opinion among the staff about my value to them as a principal negatively affected their relationships with each other, as well as with me.

My sassy statement of the issues in my rendition of Aretha Franklin's song brought the complexities of our plight at school to the surface. Honestly and boldly acknowledging the problems our entire school community faced because there was a question about my efficacy brought us an important step closer to a solution.

Working Through Conflict

Before we left for our vacation, I had worked up to swimming a mile each day. In Big Tree Calaveras State Park, I couldn't make much progress upriver, as others were doing. I swam as hard as I could, just to maintain my position in the river. I began to doubt my swimming ability and was later consoled to hear that the altitude often affected people's stamina. Different contexts may greatly affect one's ability to perform as one did elsewhere.

(Excerpted and adapted from
the August 1996 "Welcome Back"
letter I wrote to the school community)

SAVING FACE

In my first principalship, after I physically forced Carl into the building on the first day, students were probably confused to hear me say that they had to work out their differences by "using their words." Students knew that if there was a fight or altercation, they would all wind up sitting in my office and talking with each other about their conflict. Over time, they accepted this method. Sometimes I would even be approached by a student with a request to have time in my office with another student, to talk things out.

I became known for this strategy of conflict resolution, although it was incongruent with the way I had conducted myself on opening day. That first day I had done what I thought Eva or Sam would have done, not what I, Susan, would have done under any other circumstances. As administrators, it is crucial that we walk our talk, and I imagine it took me some time to earn my reputation as a caring principal who wouldn't tolerate violence or aggressive behaviors by anyone, including myself.

There were many people in the school community who did not agree with my ideas about discipline. In fact, one parent spoke directly with the superintendent, asking, "Why did you hire her to be the principal, if she won't even hit the kids when they're bad? I told her to just give him a few whacks and he'd behave, and she just won't do it!"

There were several times during my first few months when students also were surprised by the way I helped them solve problems without punishing them. They would tilt their heads in delighted disbelief as they asked, "Are you sure you're the principal?"

One night, during a concert in our school, there was a heated argument between two young men outdoors, near the very steps where Carl and I had faced off on that first day of school. Dick, the evening custodian, had been vocal in the past about his fear that he would have to take responsibility for things that weren't really his job because I wouldn't be able to do them. Sure enough, Dick came to tell me about this fight, muttering about supposing he would have to handle it.

This time I responded differently than I did on that first day, although I was plenty scared. I went outdoors, trying to look taller than my true height. Two older adolescents were yelling at each other, flaunting their bravado. I managed to ask what was happening without my voice audibly reflecting the shaking that was going on inside my body. The crowd had parted when I approached. Clearly people were watching to see what I would do with these high-school-age boys, whom I didn't know. I told them that I couldn't have them fighting outside the school and didn't want them to take their fight elsewhere either because I didn't want anyone to get hurt. "I know I could call the police, but I'd rather not do that," I continued.

With some muttering and posturing, they lowered their voices. I coaxed, "Won't you please come inside and enjoy the concert? It's actually quite good." Once I had gotten them to stop fighting, I reasoned that they might respond better if I invited them in without trying to use the power of my position to get them to act. Had I insisted on their doing what I said, I would have run the risk of creating a new confrontation—with me. By making the choice theirs, I gave them a face-saving way to stop fighting. Sometimes that's all people need to extricate themselves. When people can't see another way, they may feel they have no other choice than to fight.

I must admit to being surprised by how quickly one of the young men responded to my offer to come into the school. Smiling sheepishly, he seemed relieved to have an excuse to avoid the big confrontation that had seemed inevitable only minutes earlier.

As we walked into the school, I couldn't help but glance at Dick, having shown him and everyone else that there was more than one way to deal with a situation. I could use reason. I didn't need to intimidate people physically. Actually, I let my size and gender work to my advantage in this situation. I knew that the young men would not feel physically threatened by me, so they could respond to my invitation without worrying that anyone would think they had been coerced.

There are many ways that a leader could handle this situation, and they all could be successful. What is most important is not the particular strategy I chose, but that it was congruent with my values—it was authentic.

Of course, had both of them been truly invested in fighting and hurting each other, my strategy might not have worked. Then I would have had to resort to calling the police, because this time I obviously would not have been able to carry anyone anywhere. With so many people questioning my capability, times like these were evidence that I could lead effectively, and sometimes I needed to see the evidence as much as they did.

Taking walks with students when they were sent to me for misbehavior was another strategy I developed on the job. As we walked outside, I could see the tension melt from the students' bodies. They talked more freely about their feelings and seemed to be more open to thinking of alternative strategies for future situations. As the anger and frustration of the moment dissipated, and we walked side by side, we could be partners in addressing a problem.

I worked hard to communicate that being strong on the issues could include gentleness with people. The students seemed to be able to accept what I offered more readily than did many of the adults. How to work through conflicts with the staff was an even greater challenge.

THE PAIN OF OSTRACISM AND
THE POWER OF UNDERSTANDING

Did you ever have the experience in junior high school when some of the really popular kids were planning a party or choosing teams? You'd wait and hope to be invited, knowing deep inside that you probably would be left out. But there was something so tantalizing about being part of this team or group that you desperately wanted to be included. These longings from adolescence resurfaced for me the first year I was a principal.

At times, the staff acted like cliques of adolescents, sanctioning someone who didn't adopt their ways of doing things. I had the feeling that some of the staff members had made a pact to get rid of me. Because I dealt with conflict in a way that was unfamiliar to them, they may have felt the need to take their dissatisfaction underground. Their anger leaked out through passively hostile behavior.

The year that I arrived, the number of after-school social events among the staff seemed to increase constantly. They would have dinner, go shopping, and take day trips together. Being excluded from these events was not a problem, because I never expected or wished to take part.

Then the teachers started having more social activities at school. The most obvious additions were gourmet lunches during their lunch hour. They brought in tempting delicacies they had prepared at home and heated them in the faculty room toaster ovens. Fantastic smells wafted down the halls of the building and enticed everyone to want some of what smelled so good.

All the adults in the building were invited to attend these fabulous feasts, everyone except me. At first, I couldn't believe that I had been omitted on purpose. I told myself that maybe they had forgotten to invite me in the scurry of all the preparations. When it happened again and again, I knew that I was excluded by design.

This may not have been so unbearable if it had been restricted to lunchtime, but the event literally went on all day, what with the advance preparations, announcements of the menu, smells working their way toward everyone's noses, and then the exclamations of praise and the requests for recipes that followed. It's a wonder that the students and I could get anything done those days.

I simply couldn't comprehend that people—that teachers— would be so purposefully hurtful. "They must really hate me to do such a thing" was what kept coming to mind. I tried to tell myself that I was not in junior high and that I needed to rise above their pettiness and remember why it was happening. Yet I felt so distinctly isolated and rejected that this was hard to remember. My mind tried to reassure me, but I still felt the pain of their exclusion.

It is often said that it's lonely at the top. In my case, I didn't feel lonely from being at the top, because they were making me feel like I was at the bottom of the heap, and I was letting them. I tried to reassure myself by focusing on the inappropriateness of their expectations, but I often was overwhelmed by the feeling that my efforts to create a sense of community among such diverse and often antagonistic members of the staff were futile.

It was clear that, to many, my presence was more of an irritant than a unifying catalyst. I was not the principal anyone expected. I was not male, not middle-aged, and not physically imposing. Could a real principal be female, young, and petite—or atypical in other ways—and be accepted? Could I ever be seen as worthy or would I always remain an aberration, maybe even a fraud, in the estimation of others?

It was imperative that I get other perspectives and also that I make other lunch plans. I couldn't always get support from outside allies while I was at school. I knew I needed to give it to myself. Between the encouraging words of my allies and my own continuous affirming self-talk, I managed to keep going back to work each day.

In addition to the pain I was experiencing, there were negative consequences for others as well. The staff members were spending a great deal of time and energy planning ways to unnerve me and challenge my leadership. When people's energies are directed toward hurting another, the hostile environment that is created poisons the atmosphere for everyone. Resources squandered on negativity are not available for positive outcomes for students, families, and the staff themselves. I believe we all suffered.

It was probably at about that time that I read this statement: "Our enemies are our greatest opportunity for growth." I remember silently shouting back, "Yeah, if they don't kill you first!" But the more I thought about enemies presenting chances to grow, the truer it seemed to become. Although it was difficult to sort out at the time, those awful episodes at school were an important part of my development as a leader. I needed to think more about the forces that were driving the teachers to treat me the way they did.

Their fantasies about my lifestyle reflected, and may even have fueled, their impression that I was larger than life, or better than they were. By orchestrating these luncheons, they had created a way to knock me down to size and reclaim their desired social position. Week after week they made themselves the center of attention, and I was alone.

Although what they did was hurtful, I felt better when I began to see that it was a defense against their own confusion or uncertainty. If they didn't know what to expect at the school since I had become the principal, then at least they could control the guest list for their luncheons. When I grasped how threatened they felt, they seemed much more vulnerable to me, which eased my own defensiveness.

I began to realize that their actions wouldn't have hurt me as much if I had not continued to be so invested in belonging. It is an understandable wish, yet when it became clear that building community would be a long-term project, I had to let go of my immediate yearnings and examine the group dynamics of our school. It is crucial that a leader be able to analyze group interactions and to plan based on these dynamics. My experiences my first year pushed me to learn how to do this more quickly than I might otherwise have done. I became more adept at anticipating people's reactions and strategizing how to approach situations accordingly.

Although I had come to that school anticipating that we would all work together for the good of the students, teachers frequently had discussions about things they didn't want me to hear. Likewise, as a principal, I needed to maintain confidentiality, either to protect personnel or to respect people's wishes to keep private what they told me. Not being able to speak about these things also contributed to my feeling of being removed. Thanks to the training I got in my first year, in what felt to me like boot camp, I have been able to understand the separation that sometimes exists between staff and myself with much less angst. When I faltered, I would call to mind my friend Betty, a powerful school superintendent. She had once introduced me to a colleague of hers who had been dubbed by staff as an "FOB," which she offhandedly explained was "Friend of Betty." Instead of being hurt by this label given to anyone who enjoyed her company, Betty got a kick out of it.

Over time, I have learned that I can do what I think is right because I don't have to be held hostage by my wish to be liked by the teachers or by my fear of their rejection. Of course I still prefer that people like me, but I know that if I could survive the "gourmet lunch bunch" my first year, I can do what I have to do despite the social pressures staff or parents in the community might exert.

KNOWING WHEN TO HOLD AND WHEN TO FOLD

In my first principalship, sometimes even the simplest things I had written in memos to the staff were misunderstood and became cause for uproar. I was concerned that misunderstandings were preventing us from building the rapport and trust that I knew were essential to a good working relationship.

My solution, at the time, was to post the memos in the front office of our school. I reasoned that if the teachers read them there, the secretary or I would be able to clarify any misunderstandings on the spot and prevent the permutations that seemed to develop as the memos were discussed in the faculty lounge.

What I didn't understand was that the real issue was new leadership and people's feelings about it, rather than any misunderstanding about the content of the memos. Therefore, searching for a solution about memos would never be the answer.

Just as I thought that posting the memos had solved the problem I perceived, the situation escalated. The staff wanted copies of all the memos. At first I felt thwarted by their request, because the whole idea was to have the teachers read the memos in the office, where either the secretary or I was present. I began to sense that the teachers wanted copies of the memos to collect "evidence" about me. I refused. After so many other slights, this was the last straw. Unfortunately, I had chosen the wrong time to stand firm and assert myself.

I said that we were a small staff and there was no reason to make copies of these memos. I told them I thought it would be more communal to have a central place where people could read them. It was a mistake, though, to oppose what they said they needed. To justify their demand, they countered that there were things they were required to do in response to the memos, so they needed copies as reminders. I said that they could take notes from the memo that was posted in the office. We now battled over my refusal to respond to their request for copies. I weakly said that I didn't want to waste paper. Then, when I put little notes on students' lockers asking them to please close their locker doors, the teachers countered that because I used paper to write notes to the students, why wouldn't I copy memos for them? I quickly asserted that I thought there was a difference between children and adults. We were in a battle that never should have happened, but I couldn't see my way out.

A confidant outside school suggested that I not use memos to share information. Why not have morning meetings to share the contents of the proposed memos and thereby sidestep posting or duplicating the information? I implemented this idea immediately, in the hope of extricating myself from this tug-of-war. The way I jumped at this idea reminds me of the boy outside our school who was so ready to accept my invitation to come inside because he really didn't want to fight. I didn't want to fight either, but I felt that my authority was being tested and I had chosen not to back down. I had to learn the hard way that this was not the way to win anything, least of all respect.

I began to have grade-level meetings every few days to talk with teachers about school issues or whatever else required their input, but their response was less than positive. Now, I surely can see their point. They were being coerced to attend these meetings. They and I both knew it. Although they had to come, they couldn't be made to like it or to participate in a dialogue, so it became a monologue, with me talking and them seething.

My inexperience was further exemplified by my indecisiveness about incoming mail. Because I was new, I wasn't sure which mail was important and which could go immediately to the "round file." At these morning meetings, I sometimes would mention something, such as an educational contest, that came in the mail and ask teachers' opinions about whether we should have our students participate. One teacher later characterized these morning meetings as "Susan reading the mail to us." Her words stung, not only because they trivialized my intent for these meetings, but also because there was an element of truth in what she said. An experienced principal would have been able to sort through these offers and decide whether any were worth pursuing.

Although I spent a lot of time being angry with the teachers for being so unfair and unresponsive, I realized that if I wanted to be effective I needed to understand them. They clearly were not interested in walking a mile in my moccasins. I would have to walk in theirs. True leadership can happen only if people are willing to join the leader, and that also requires that the leader do the joining.

I couldn't make the teachers respect me, and my invalidation of their feelings clearly was having the opposite effect. Now I know that articulating my understanding of another's feelings is a much better way to invite a dialogue, even when the conversation may be about differences of opinion. I can try to justify my own feelings and my actions, although what I did was really very silly. It was important to realize that I was getting stuck in a situation I simply could not change. The teachers' behavior in this situation was about my newness. I couldn't rush the process of our getting to know each other, no matter how intolerable I found the teachers' behavior to be.

Sometimes leaders can make a situation feel more bearable by remembering that people's actions often are not as "personal" as they may seem. I wish I had known more about group dynamics when I entered this principalship. Even though I knew a lot about teaching and had worked in a family business for many years, I was not prepared well enough to understand the complex interactions in our school from an administrative perspective. By taking graduate courses in educational administration, I learned about some of the forces that were driving the very things I was experiencing at work. I also had the camaraderie of other administrators, which enabled me to distance myself from the situations and realize that some of the dynamics were predictable, regardless of the individuals involved. These insights helped me grow in my ability to grapple with challenges more objectively, rather than feeling them quite so personally.

WHAT'S WORTH FIGHTING FOR

All of a sudden, students were being sent to the front office for disciplinary reasons at a phenomenal rate. At first there were 10 of them, and then the crowd thickened to many more. The reasons the teachers wrote on the office referral notes seemed insignificant, and the students were boisterous and indignant about being sent to see me. What should I do? What would you do if 50 kids suddenly appeared in the front office?

I had implemented a system for discipline that required any student sent to the office to complete a form before seeing me. The students had to respond to three questions: What happened? How do you feel about it now? Is there anything else you want to tell me?

The secretary was busy giving out these forms to the students. The office clerk was furiously trying to provide pencils for all the students who needed them; our pencil sharpener had never seen such action. In fact, we had never seen this many people in the front office at one time. It seemed highly implausible that everyone had misbehaved at exactly 2:00 p.m., 1 hour before school was to be dismissed.

I had to spend some time figuring out which of the students were involved in the same incident, so this sorting process used up some of the hour that I had left. I tried to see as many groups of students as possible, but they all left at dismissal time to board their buses, and I was left to make sense of this mess. I stayed at the office and telephoned each student at home to hear what had happened. By 10:00 p.m., I had spoken to every student involved, and felt reasonably sure that none of them had done anything terribly wrong. In fact, I questioned why they had been sent to see me at all.

The next morning I heard what really happened from a staff member who wasn't a teacher. The teachers had agreed they each would send five students to the office at the appointed hour to see how I would handle the situation, and all but one teacher did. At the time, I felt like I had only one ally among all the classroom teachers. Were there no other teachers courageous enough to defy peer pressure? Were there no others who could put the children's needs first? What they did was outrageous. Experience had not prepared me to deal with this situation. Still, I wonder whether any experienced principals have ever faced this situation, and what they did.

I did not confront the teachers with what they had done. If they could use their students to express their own feelings about me as a principal, I was fearful that to engage the teachers would be to further entangle the students in this war-zone mentality in our school. As much as I wanted justice, I felt protective of the students, so I tried to deal with the presenting situation as best I could and move forward.

I wasn't allowed to move forward. A few days later, several students came to my office in tears. They said that they were studying democracy and that their teacher had told them the way they could learn more about it was to circulate a petition among the students in the school. The petition said that I was a bad principal and should be fired. These girls were crying because they didn't want to collect signatures from their peers to fulfill their assignment.

I can't believe I didn't confront the teacher about this contemptuous behavior and mockery of democracy. The students were the ones who actually showed the most courage in this situation. After reassuring them that I wouldn't be fired, I once again went about my business. I think I was trying to hide, perhaps from myself, how publicly shamed I felt that a teacher in our school would involve students in a vendetta against me. Such a despicable act certainly revealed a great deal of contempt for me. I tried not to let on to the staff how enraged and vulnerable I felt. I'm sure I also felt paralyzed by the abusiveness of the situation, as well as by my confusion about how things could get to such a fevered pitch.

When the teachers summoned union leadership from the state level to support a grievance they were filing, I actually was relieved. I thought that an objective union staff member would help the teachers put things in perspective. Instead, this person was very cavalier about the events at our school, mocking me and playing to the teachers, who tittered at his comments. The intimidation and ridicule by the state union representative left me feeling beaten down and gun-shy about confronting the teachers again, which was exactly his goal.

While the teachers went out for drinks together after these episodes, I went home alone. My whole focus at that time revolved around my job. Because I was new to the area, it was taking time to make new friends and establish a local support network. My feelings of isolation made the teachers' strategy at work all the more effective.

So I guess it's not surprising that I simply refused to engage the teacher about the horrifying, mean-spirited behavior with the petition. I was afraid that naming it might cause a further downward spiral, yet I knew that ignoring it wasn't right either. As a "good woman" and a "good principal," I was trying to "make nice," remain calm, and find a peaceful settlement. There were serious consequences to my choosing such a path.

What still bothers me the most about not handling that situation well is that I didn't attend to the students' needs. I clearly had been intimidated by this scandalous behavior. Students must have had a lot of questions about what was happening, and some of the youngsters clearly were distressed. Putting my head in the sand wasn't going to make their confusion go away. By not directly confronting the issue, I missed an important opportunity. I didn't model strength or courage.

It's hard to have courage in this kind of situation. Addressing the incident of the petition would have been like putting kerosene on a flame. Because I wanted to avoid an explosion, I was reluctant to make that choice. I felt like a hostage in an unstable environment in which there was no mutually agreed-upon code of ethics. The teachers' behavior in these two incidents was so heinous that I sometimes felt like I was working in a crazy place, and, like people in traumatic situations, my sleep was affected greatly. I would wake up literally every hour throughout the night, as if I needed to check my back. That's how frightening I found these school experiences.

I couldn't imagine the teachers doing this to each other. Was their behavior because I was the principal or was it driven by their reaction to my personality or my approach to leadership? Did it have anything to do with my being a woman who was relatively young? They hadn't done this to previous principals, yet they had not had a principal who was nontraditional. I had never encountered this kind of treatment before from colleagues, and I needed to understand it.

DIVERSITY IN THE PRINCIPAL'S OFFICE

Women are expected to attend to others' needs, and in fact are sometimes criticized when they put their own needs or ideas first. As a result, women often swallow their voices and try to keep the peace. Although I struggled to be perceived as a leader who spoke up, my uncertainty was probably evident. I had temporarily lost my voice.

I'm not sure how I managed to keep persevering in the face of the animosity I experienced, but I was determined not to leave without having had a fair chance to succeed at what I was trying to do. It was obvious that what I had hoped to achieve at the grade-level meetings I had initiated was missing the point. So I scrapped the meetings, gave copies of the memo to each teacher, and moved on.

My thinking about leadership when I began my principalship was much more about the traits necessary to do the job than the characteristics of the individual in it. I've come to understand that the gender of the person in the position may have a strong effect on how that person's behaviors are perceived by the different constituencies. In some people's opinion, he is assertive; she's aggressive. He is passionate; she's hysterical. He has idiosyncrasies; she's crazy.

Women aren't the only targets. I believe that every person of minority status has been subjected to perceptions that reflect a double standard. Minorities and people who are atypical in any visible way very often are observed with a more critical eye by some percentage of their constituency. Even if it is only a small number of people who are unsupportive in this way, their judgments sting.

For me, the most obvious ways that I was different were gender and age. Many people equate leadership so much with being male that, when asked to list as many leaders as possible in a given amount of time, every group I know of has listed mostly, if not all, men—white men. For many, white men remain the leaders and women and other minorities the caretakers.

Yet even when women or other minorities are the leaders, do some of us try to be more like the white males they see in the role? I was aware of possible criticisms when I engaged with the students in childlike play. I initially felt compelled to wear dark suits, rather than more bold colors and patterns. And when I designed my office to be warm and inviting, many people seemed confused by an atmosphere they didn't associate with "the principal's office." We grapple with these issues in our own careers, and as educators we have a responsibility to help students broaden their thinking, both as they view others and as they contemplate their own roles and futures.

ESTABLISHING CREDIBILITY

Throughout my career I have wanted to help students clarify their beliefs and use their voices and their behaviors to assert themselves. An experience I had later in my career was an excellent opportunity for me to do just that. The fifth-grade teachers and I had taken all of the fifth graders on a three-day team-building experience. I was to chaperone some of the girls for the two nights we were there. It was 9:00 p.m. when I approached the cabin of my 11 charges, and I did not like what I saw. The girls were gyrating their hips and giggling as they beckoned to the boys in the adjacent cabin. Although the girls were laughing, I thought this was serious. This was about role perceptions and belonging. The girls were inviting a reaction from the boys, but I knew they needed one from me as well.

"Stop," I called to them, but they continued. My middle-aged self was thinking, "I'm getting too old for this." I quickened my pace and kept calling to them, but they kept shaking and waving to the boys. Then I saw Amy doing a shimmy and there was even more shouting and laughing. By this time, I was angry about being ignored, and I walked up behind her and said in a stern voice, "Get in the cabin. All of you." Amy almost jumped out of her skin, and then everyone went inside. After a few minutes, I thought about how uncomfortable the girls, especially Amy, probably were about being spoken to so forcefully. What a way to start off our 5th-grade trip, a trip designed to build self-esteem through risk taking!

I found Amy and said I was sorry that I scared her, but told her of my frustration when she and the others had not responded to my four attempts to get them to stop. "We never heard you," she said, and I realized that the noise they and the boys were making probably had prevented them from hearing me.

"The real reason I was so upset," I told her in a softer voice, "was that I want you to maintain your dignity."

Amy looked puzzled and asked, "What does that mean?"

I was surprised by her question until I thought more about the words I had chosen. I wondered to myself, "These days, is dignity something 11-year-olds think about?" I was starting to feel ancient. I knew I had to pursue this because I care deeply about how emerging young women perceive themselves and present themselves to others.

I talked with Amy about how natural it was for girls to be curious about boys and for boys to be curious about girls. I understood that the girls were being a little provocative in a playful way, but I was concerned that some of their movements made me think that the girls were not maintaining respect for themselves. Amy listened carefully to what I said about dignity. Then she apologized. I appreciated that she had heard me and told her I wasn't angry with her. It wasn't a question of fault, and I wasn't looking for an apology.

A few minutes later I decided to speak with the rest of the girls, and they had the same reaction to my statement about dignity. They seemed genuinely interested when they asked, "What do you mean by maintaining our dignity?"

How could I explain this concept without the girls thinking I was referring only to wiggling their hips? I wanted the girls to understand that how they presented themselves mattered in many different situations, not just with boys.

After we talked, another girl, April, asked whether I would play "Truth or Dare" with them. I don't know whether it was the twinkle in her eye, the raised eyebrow, or the beginning of a smile, but I knew I'd be letting myself in for something. Yet I wanted to balance my initial anger with them by joining in what they wanted to do.

"Truth or Dare," I learned, is a game in which a bottle is spun and when it stops, the person it points to is asked a question or given a dare. I hesitated. To get me to play, April offered the option to "pass" if I really didn't want to respond. Although I don't favor this kind of game, I took a deep breath and cautiously said I would play. After talking about dignity and my values, I wanted to hear what went through their minds.

The first thing April wanted me to do (after she manipulated the bottle so that it pointed to me) was to go up to the lamp and make believe I was dancing with it as if it were a boy. She whispered to friends that she wanted me to dance in a "sexy" way. I'm not sure whether the girls were tittering about her audacity in asking me, about the thought of my being seductive with a lamp—or anyone, for that matter—or out of nervousness about what I might say or do. When I refused to dance seductively with the lamp, April walked right up to me and put her face in mine. Ignoring the fact that she had been the one to assure me I could pass, she taunted me, "Chicken, chicken, what's the matter, are you a chicken?"

Although it was shocking that a student would act this way with the principal of her school, April had a history of being candid, and she knew what she could expect from me, even if she did something that I found unacceptable. Even though I was more than 30 years older than April, and the principal of her school, part of me still felt pressured by her dare.

I asked incredulously, "Do you really think that I will be intimidated by you calling me a chicken? I'm not going to do something I don't want to, just because you are teasing me." After I said that I wouldn't do it, I thought more about April's peers. If it took a bit of strength for me to defy her command, I could only imagine how difficult it would be for her friends. April could be very convincing.

I had several choices about how to respond. I could have been indignant and refused to put up with that kind of behavior, or I could have reminded April that she had offered me the option to pass. Both choices would have sidestepped the real issue and I would have missed a chance to interact meaningfully with the girls. For me, this was an opportunity to model a way to refuse to do something. I could show the girls how setting limits was one way I maintained my dignity, and I hoped to empower them to set their own limits.

"I don't think your friends will always do what you want them to do either," I said to April. My motivation was neither to divide and conquer nor to put April down. Her friends should have a true choice if they were dared to do something. I wanted to add possibilities to their options and to give them permission to do what they really wanted.

I also hoped to give April a chance to learn how to deal with a challenge to her social authority. April had trusted me enough to risk dropping her student-to-principal mask and to speak with me directly. I believe she knew that I would not "pull rank" and hide from her challenge by using my institutional power. She knew that I would show my respect for her regardless of what she said. If there was any power I would call upon, it would be my personal power, which came from my own self-respect and dignity.

April did get some other girls to go up to the lamp, but when they got there, they asked her what they should do. She demonstrated and they tried to imitate her or did their own dance. I wondered, with a bit of worry, what prompted April to do this, but I knew that my immediate response needed to focus on the dynamic among the girls and on dignity and decision making.

Although her voice was tentative, one girl, Jenna, did refuse to do the dance. She looked at me, as if to get confirmation that she didn't have to do it, just as I had chosen not to. By seeing me model assertiveness and communicate my feelings, Jenna was able to state her own refusal. Had I used my age or institutional power as the basis of my response to April, Jenna would not have seen something she could do also.

As quickly as all of this started, it was interrupted when Danielle asked whether she could put makeup on me. Perhaps she was getting bored with the whole game and was ready for a change, or was Danielle trying to avoid an inevitable confrontation between April and Jenna about the dare? Did Danielle sense the need to discharge the situation in which April and I held opposite points of view? If I allowed Danielle to put makeup on me, none of the other girls would be in the position of having to choose to comply with or defy April's dare. Instead of being in a situation in which we were at odds, we could all join together. I wondered whether Danielle's idea subtly gave more credence to my thinking by making me the center of attention. (Danielle had asked to put makeup on me, not on everyone.)

I could have chosen to bring the girls back to the issue by suggesting we continue playing "Truth or Dare," but sometimes leadership is as much about knowing when to drop something as when to make a lesson out of it. Sometimes "less is more."

Danielle's request to make me up also took me by surprise, although it didn't feel nearly as risky as April's request. I stalled for time by asking, "Do you intend to wear all that when you climb the high ropes tomorrow?" Her friends laughed and told me that she brings makeup with her all the time, just to play with. It is often younger girls who put on makeup just for fun, and I couldn't help but be amused by how these girls were fluctuating between acting both older and younger than their actual ages.

The girls roared with laughter as they fought to put the makeup on me in exaggerated proportions. When they were finished, they decided that I looked quite good and advised me to wear more makeup to school. "Oh, you think so, do you?" I responded, and we laughed about whether that was actually advice I would take. I was struck by the fact that I had been talking about maintaining dignity. With that overdone makeup I might not have looked very dignified, but I believe that in this interaction I was every bit the principal I wanted to be. Danielle and her friends were engaging with me by making me look different, yet ironically I was my most authentic during this encounter.

Being made up was a way in which I was willing to have the joke be on me. By laughing together and even letting them take my picture before I washed my face, I signaled that I wouldn't pull rank on them. Because I was feeling comfortable with myself, there was no contradiction between being firm about things that mattered and then being playful at other times. In both cases, I maintained my personal and professional dignity.

The girls responded to my firmness about dignity because they could sense that it was important and that I shared it because I cared about them. I believe some of the girls wanted to learn how to be assertive, so they focused on my example to try it on for size. They wanted to understand beauty, so they experimented with makeup and its effect on my looks. They had to be fairly comfortable with me to do this. Later that night, I told the girls that if they were upset or didn't feel well, I would not mind if they woke me up at any time. They seemed comforted and pleased. I was their mother away from home. When I wanted them to respect themselves and their bodies, they seemed interested in my opinion, although it clearly came from someone of a different generation. Yet when it came to playing with makeup, we could bridge the age difference and giggle together about how I looked. Perhaps that is why I let them do it.

In this interaction, we stepped beyond our roles of student and principal. The girls' spontaneity and candor enhanced my understanding of them. My efforts to hear them and join them, while being myself, were what gave me influence with them, and together we could all explore some of the issues we face as females: assertiveness, attractiveness, dignity, and conviction.

I believe that communication is most effective when there is a sense of mutuality between the people in the relationship. When we are in a dialogue with people with whom we share common interests or concerns, even if we disagree about appropriate courses of action, we are most apt to hear each other.

In my discussion with the girls, I rejected the use of power based on my position or age. Instead, I made a choice to relate to them by finding common ground, thinking they would be more receptive to sharing their thoughts and beliefs with me, and hearing mine.

I had found a way to relate to the girls that worked for us. Another leader may have established mutuality differently. As long as leaders communicate in ways that are congruent with their beliefs and the situation, the interactions are likely to be much more meaningful.

LESSONS LEARNED

One of the biggest responsibilities I felt as a leader was the impact of what I said and did, both in the moment of the interaction with the person or people involved and in the message it sent to others. I don't think that the specifics of what I did in different circumstances mattered as much as whether I tried to understand people's needs and respond to them, and whether I was trusted. When I was with the girls in the cabin, to be most effective I had to be inside the situation, responding as an individual, as well as outside it, cognizant of the effect of my words and actions as a principal with her students.

I did not always consider this duality, but after years of experience I have learned that if I respond authentically to a situation, it often turns out to be effective for a broader lesson as well. The girls in the cabin knew me and already had decided that I could be trusted. The young men about to have a fight the night of the concert may have taken a chance with me because I showed that I was aware of some of their needs and willing to join them in exploring alternatives. In each situation, I was able to use my influence as a leader because of three things: concern, understanding of needs, and trust. In the struggle about the memos, I came to understand that the staff's mistrust of me reflected their fears and anger and the futility of battling about the posting of daily messages. I was then able to let go, to get outside the situation, and begin to defuse it. Another person might say and do things differently in any of these situations, and it could be equally meaningful as long as it was genuine.

One of the mistakes of leadership is not knowing when to push and when to let go. When I didn't address the situation about the petition against me, I let something go that I shouldn't have. When I insisted that the memos be posted in the office, I pushed when I should have let go. When Danielle changed the course of events by suggesting she put makeup on me, I think I got the balance right by going with the flow.

When I think of conflict and leadership, I often think of the difference between an Eastern and Western way of dealing with force. If a person pushes us and we try to hold our ground, as a Westerner may do, we may fall over. If we take the energy that comes at us and move with it fluidly, as an Easterner may do, we might maintain our balance. Resisting may feel good for the ego, but it doesn't usually work in the long run. Of course there are circumstances in which a firm refusal is the only appropriate response. Wisely assessing the situation, which may be unfolding very quickly, is what a leader needs to do.

As leaders, we must find ways to maintain the vision of our school community, while dealing with the conflicts that inevitably arise among its members. If we find ourselves directly involved in the conflict, we have to consider our actions, both as participant and as leader of the school. We may need to take a more global view of the impact of the conflict on others and act accordingly.

Sometimes individual needs conflict with the practices of the school community. In those situations, a leader's acknowledgment of the feelings, as well as a restatement of the guiding principles, may be the best course of action.

CHAPTER THREE

Communicating Who We Are and What We Believe

A dear friend gave me a calendar as a gift to mark the new year. I scratched my head in puzzlement when I saw the cover picture of a scantily clad woman who was mountain climbing. What on earth was my friend thinking when she selected this for me? She was surprised that it hadn't been obvious to me. "You have been a mentor, a coach to me in so many ways. I remember you struggling with things that seemed insurmountable, and then using those accomplishments to fortify you for your next endeavors. I can actually hear you urging me to do what I need to do, with full confidence that I will be successful. Of course I chose the 'Women Who Climb' calendar for you. I don't care what that woman was wearing; she represented how you challenge yourself and others to go the next step."

USING SYMBOLS TO CONVEY VALUES

Symbols are powerful leadership tools. In my three principalships, I have found that symbols can be used to announce or emphasize important messages to the school community.

When I walked into what was to be my office in my first princi-palship, I encountered a barricade. The former principal had arranged a large, gray metal desk and two gray filing cabinets in a row, facing the entrance to the office. I knew I couldn't work in such a setting, so I decided to tear it down and build one that I thought would be right for all of us in the school community. Although I wasn't sure exactly what it would be, I did know that I wanted an office that was welcoming and warm and that would be comfortable for me and anyone who joined me in it.

In the spirit of finding a way to make my office reflect my style, I set about to find some wooden furniture, scouring the attics and storage rooms of many of the schools and the administration build-ing. Some administrators were confused by my unwillingness to accept their generous offers to order some new metal office furniture.

Eventually I pieced together just what I wanted. I placed a refin-ished oak desk at a diagonal to the doorway, with a chair to the side of the desk; peering over a desk was not the way I wanted to begin conversations. Then I bought a braided rug on which I put oak chairs in an oval configuration. Floor lamps, braided chair pads, a tapestry, and student artwork added the aesthetic quality I desired.

I had created a warm environment, where the furniture and how it was arranged conveyed an invitation for conversation. Authoritarian power was not the message I wanted people to receive as they entered my office. I was beginning to tell people how I envi-sioned connecting with the members of our school community.

In another school where I became the principal, youngsters would stand and patiently wait behind a front office counter that was so high that the adults on the other side didn't even know some-one was there. When I began that principalship, I had a section of that counter cut out so that it would be evident immediately that a child was on the other side. This work order was one of the most important actions I took as principal in my first year there. It told the community that I valued the kindergartners as much as the 6th-graders, and that the physical setup of our school would accommo-date the 5-year-olds as well as it served the 12-year-olds and adults.

Desks and counters are not the only things that can keep people apart. I recall when Gina asked me about the coffee fund at the first faculty meeting of one of my new principalships. I was a little bewildered.

I replied, "I don't drink coffee myself, but I'll be happy to con-tribute if that's the way you do things here."

Because I looked puzzled by her first question, Gina clarified, "How are we going to handle the coffee each day?"

I still didn't get it. "What do you mean?"

"Well," Gina said, "the principal used to set up the arrangements for who would make the coffee and how we would collect the money."

I didn't know whether I was more shocked or amused. "Listen, how you work that out among yourselves is up to you. I don't think I need to have anything to do with that, do you?"

Gina was a congenial person, and she looked at me for a minute to weigh my response. I think it was when she decided I was being forthright that she said a little sheepishly, "This all may seem strange to you, but we are used to the principal telling us how she wants all these things done."

I knew I didn't have to be in charge of something the teachers easily could do themselves, and changing the protocol was a way to signal that my leadership wouldn't include micromanagement.

In another school, our logo told a great deal about our beliefs. I had decided that we needed a school logo to put on our stationery and publications, and that the students should be involved in creating it. We decided to have a contest to choose the logo. Our art teacher offered to teach about logos in art classes on every grade level. Design teams of several students each were formed in every class and they worked on entries to the contest.

A panel of adult judges viewed the many logos, which were posted on display boards in the school lobby. Eventually, a logo created by two kindergarten students was selected.

Ironically, some kindergartners initially had objected to participating in the contest because they assumed that adult judges would think that the art of older children was better. One of the things that the judges found appealing about the winning entry, in fact, was that it wasn't overly polished. You could tell that more than one child did the drawing; the arms drawn at each end of the row of people were depicted differently. No one pointed this out because no one wanted it to be "corrected." This reflects the philosophy of acceptance and appreciation that the school community had worked to develop and honor. The differences in the picture didn't exclude it as a viable entry; in fact, they made it more charming.

Rather than using some official-looking seal as our logo, we used this picture of three smiling children, symbolizing that children are the core of our school community. We wanted everyone to know

Figure 3.1   The Thoreau School logo. Created by Will Haver and
Meaghan Kilian.

that children were our primary focus, and I believe our logo was a constant reminder.

Leaders utilize symbols to convey, simply, what is often the most complex. Visual symbols can be easily understood and remembered, and they even can be used to articulate a school philosophy. People must know about the institutions that are significant in their lives, and leaders must use every possible vehicle to communicate their message.

Communicating our message as leaders includes being aware of how we use our faces and bodies.

SHE SMILES TOO MUCH

My smile has been a source of attention since I was young. In fact, in those early days, I took offense each time someone complimented my smile. There was a reason for my reaction. My younger brother was adorable, and people would stop my mother on the street to comment on his big blue eyes and happy demeanor. After gushing about Paul, they would notice me. The big grins on their faces would start to fade, and they would invariably say something like, "Oh, she's cute too. . . . She has a nice smile." Their expressions convinced me that they were searching for something polite to say about me after fawning over my brother. "They talk like I'm a horse that has good teeth," I complained to my mother each time it happened.

As I got older, I felt even more uncertain about my appearance. Being an adolescent can be difficult anyway, and having a very appealing younger sibling didn't help my self-confidence. One time when I was moping around the house, my mother advised me, "You ought to smile. Nobody likes to be with a sourpuss." I took her words to heart, especially because at that age I was particularly vulnerable to the thought of not being popular. I smiled more often, and, like whistling in the dark, it became a habit that enabled me to feel more at ease.

Years later, I was startled when someone I had just met at a dinner party asked me whether I had worn braces as a child. "What gives you that idea?" I asked incredulously.

"Well, you seem to keep your lips closed when you smile. People often acquire that habit when they wear braces." I was dumbfounded by his observation. After years of being noticed for my smile, now I had been noticed for concealing it.

Thinking about it, I realized that unpleasant experiences at work were probably affecting my smile. I vividly remembered times when I sat in school committee meetings and listened to the newly elected chairperson criticize me for things that had nothing to do with my behavior as a principal. I painfully recalled how aware I was of my appearance as she spoke. Frankly, I didn't know what to do with my face. What she was saying was untrue and vindictive, yet I didn't want to show how hurt I was by her comments. That would have given her more power.

I was being shamed publicly and I imagined people were looking at me to gauge my reaction to her remarks. When people would catch my eye and smile sympathetically, I felt awkward smiling back, yet didn't want to cry either. The compromise I worked out, without much thought at the time, was to smile with my lips closed.

Becoming an administrator opened me to a level of scrutiny that was daunting. It seemed that everything I did was being observed and analyzed. It became clear that I would never please everyone with anything that I did. This seems obvious, yet because I was on the receiving end of the disapproval it was hard for me to take the criticisms in stride. I needed to remember that I couldn't please all the people all the time, although the teachers clearly expected me to please each of them.

In one meeting with the superintendent, each teacher came prepared to share a gripe about me. I was most stunned when one teacher hurled the accusation, "She smiles too much." When I told friends about it later, they saw the comment as an example of a teacher lamely searching to find something negative to say about me, and coming up with only this silly judgment. I wondered if they were put off by me reflecting an emotion that didn't match the way they were feeling.

Being publicly shamed had a deep impact on me. I worked very hard to conceal my pain and found ways to arrange my face that kept people from knowing my true feelings. This worked on some levels, in that it didn't reveal how wounded I felt by these unwarranted attacks, but it came with a price. In the process of managing my outward appearance, I was losing track of what was happening for me inside.

Choosing more neutral expressions also denied others the information that might have led some of them to offer me support. There surely have been those who have seen beyond my facade or listened as I spoke with them candidly about how I really felt. Their empathy and support meant a great deal to me, and still does. But the price I paid for publicly appearing to be unscathed by vicious attacks was that many people never realized how deeply hurt I was and, therefore, could not respond even if they wanted to.

Because I was so concerned about the impressions that I was creating with my body language and facial expressions, it was disquieting to have that stranger comment on my smile. His speculation about braces addressed something I didn't even know I was doing. I considered myself to be very self-aware, so his comment was alarming. What else were others able to know about me that I didn't even know about myself? I worried that if I didn't know what I was doing with my own face, maybe I was also missing crucial information about others. These concerns magnified my questions about how I would be perceived.

I was trying to show others that I could do the job for which I was hired, and I didn't want anything I did to reveal my uncertainty or discomfort with any part of my job. I tried to demonstrate my competence and feared that being too honest about my confusion or ambivalence might create or reinforce the impression that I would not be a good principal, as predicted by those skeptical of my appointment. As a woman, perhaps I was concerned even more about concealing my feelings and reactions at work, not wanting to appear overemotional, as women are sometimes stereotypically portrayed.

There is another reason why leaders, both male and female, may consider carefully how much of their own emotional reactions they share with their staff. People may be concerned that we won't be able to oversee events and attend to the staff's or community members' needs while we are feeling and displaying our own emotions. In the face of other people's discomfort, we might decide not to share or process our feelings with the group. We need to resist this option. By being authentic about our feelings, as well as our thoughts, we also may make it feel safer for others to share their feelings or opinions.

Some people need to process feelings in order to participate fully in the agenda items of a meeting. Others want as little processing as possible and find it unbearable when there is anything that interferes with the action items on the agenda. If leaders want to process anything affecting their own emotional responses, there may be even more resentment from those who already have a low tolerance for process. Leaders making the choice to share their feelings with teachers, if they are feeling unfairly accused or in need of support, may result in teachers feeling obligated to respond because of the leaders' power, even if this is not the leaders' intention. The teachers may perceive that leaders are taking advantage of their role and thwarting the efforts of the group to move forward. One of a leader's most challenging tasks is to find the balance, on any given day, between a focus on the process and a focus on the outcomes. In addition, the leader's own feelings certainly affect the process of the group. This must be acknowledged.

We can predict that not everyone will agree with the way we choose to handle whether or when we share our feelings. Modeling acceptance of disagreement about how and what I processed in meetings, without being devastated by it, may have helped other colleagues learn how to handle negative feedback on choices they make. It also actually may have freed people to disagree constructively without being so concerned that they will anger or hurt the leader that they refrained from speaking.

BEING CLEAR

In addition to choices leaders face about the extent to which they share their feelings, they also need to consider the way they share their thoughts. A leader needs to be mindful of not stating an opinion so definitively that it signals that only one point of view is permissible. When the leader expresses an idea, the staff may feel that positional power punctuates the words. If the way the opinion is stated implies there is no room for disagreement, colleagues may feel shut down and collaboration will be compromised.

For example, some teachers have very strong opinions about inclusion and their responsibility to meet the needs of every student in their class. In one meeting, teachers heatedly stated that they felt that their skills and hard work were rewarded by having even more students with special needs assigned to them year after year. Inadvertently, that sometimes did happen. One teacher, Alex, proposed that all the children with special needs be put in one room, which would then have a full-time tutor to help teach the children. I responded very quickly that I couldn't live with that arrangement, because I believed it was in the best interests of the children not to be so identified and grouped.

There was mumbling, and glances were exchanged. Although some teachers continued to talk, I later learned from several staff members that many people felt that I had shut Alex down with my comment. They felt this was Susan not listening to what other people think if she doesn't agree with them. I thought a lot about the effect of my stated opinion on conversation and teacher involvement, and I discussed it with many teachers over the course of the next few weeks.

The teachers may have had many reasons for not addressing this issue with me in the meeting. Some may have feared retribution, and others may have wanted to avoid conflict among colleagues with different viewpoints. Still others simply may not have wanted to prolong the discussion.

Would it have been better to let this suggestion stay on the table, when I knew that it was a suggestion I would not be able to support? I felt that it was fairer to state from the beginning that I couldn't live with it and not let the faculty be misled. What I neglected to do was create space to discuss the problem Alex was trying to address, even though I disagreed with his suggestion.

Another time there was a discussion about the effect of tutors entering the classroom to support specific students in various subject areas. Some teachers felt it was disruptive, and they didn't want to have to teach subjects at prearranged times. They wanted the freedom to explore "teaching moments." They valued the flexibility to lengthen a lesson or to integrate different subjects and didn't want to be forced to teach in ways that made less sense to them pedagogically.

One teacher, Pat, went on to say that if what was being done was working for the majority of the children, it wasn't fair to limit a teacher because a few kids couldn't keep up and because support staff were not always available. In fact, Pat wondered whether some of the students would be better served by receiving tutoring outside the classroom, thereby eliminating the need for a teacher to adhere to a prearranged schedule of "in-class" support.

I believed we couldn't sacrifice the needs of any student in order to make it easier to teach the majority. As educators we need to think carefully about all factors and make decisions about what best serves each student, even when it is more difficult for the adults. How could I, as the leader, hold onto this belief and still encourage an open exchange?

I was determined to let people express themselves in the discussion and not to repeat previous behaviors of mine that had shut down conversation. I worked very hard to use body language that encouraged sharing. I was very aware of my facial expression. I tried to convey interest in different points of view. I refrained from reacting to each comment. Instead, I focused on giving different people opportunities to say what they thought. I even asked people whose reactions were evident by their facial expressions to tell us what they were thinking. I purposefully leaned back in my chair, hoping to encourage expression of all viewpoints.

Although I was pleased that people seemed to feel free to say what was on their minds, as they did so, I was feeling uncomfortable. Their thoughts, because they were so vehemently stated and largely unchallenged, appeared to express the majority viewpoint, and I had not voiced my disagreement.

After the meeting, the reactions were mixed. Some said it was a great meeting. Others were deeply upset by what they heard their colleagues say and because I did not challenge the opinions expressed.

I was appreciative that some of the teachers shared their reactions with me. It gave me an opportunity to explain that I had been trying to provide an outlet for their colleagues to express themselves. I told them that I was hoping that colleagues would address each other, rather than wait for me to "come down" on those speaking.

In fact, several teachers agreed that they thought it would be much more effective if teachers spoke with each other. They would rather not leave it to me and then hear the predictable response: "She's an administrator. Of course she doesn't understand." Later, I heard that a couple of staff members were specifically advising colleagues to state their thoughts and not leave it to me to say what they were thinking.

I was alarmed that some of our newer teachers, who had not previously heard me speak adamantly about our commitment to inclusion and our responsibilities to all children, felt unsupported or uncertain about where I stood on the issue. As I spoke with the ones who approached me, I urged them to speak with other colleagues if they heard anyone who had concerns similar to their own and to let them know why I allowed the conversation to flow as it did.

I knew that this was an inadequate response. I wish that I had said what I was going to do at the beginning of the meeting. I could have been open about the fact that I wanted to encourage dialogue and, therefore, would not be reacting to each comment. I would have made it clear that my silence did not connote agreement with everything said, but rather a strong desire to let different perspectives be represented.

I imagine some of the staff would have been put off by me saying that I would try not to share my reactions in an effort to promote dialogue. They may not have trusted that I would be open to their opinions because I already had a strong opinion. I would hope, however, that some teachers remembered times when I changed my mind after listening to their convincing arguments.

A central consideration in this instance was whether the issue could be debated and decided accordingly, or whether, in fact, the law dictated a certain course of action. In retrospect, I think that I would have been more effective if I had paraphrased their different points of view and then stated the law as I understood it. I think such an approach would have been more effective because it would have made it clear that some decisions were not ours to make. In this case, the law could speak for itself.

EXPRESSING OUTRAGE

I remember a time when there was a big commotion after recess because a student had pulled down another student's shorts while they were playing outside. After hearing from the recess supervisors and the classroom teachers, I interviewed each of the identified students individually. Daniel readily admitted his guilt and the seriousness of his offense. He already understood why what he had done was wrong. As he took responsibility for his misbehavior, he confided, "I know I shouldn't have done it. But they were saying, 'Do it! Do it!' and after a while I just gave in."

The other students who were involved all pointed fingers at each other, but only Patrick admitted he was part of the group that goaded Daniel to "pants" the other child. After consulting with several colleagues in our school, I took a very strong position. I punished all the children involved to the same degree.

I told them that Daniel did something very wrong, admitted his wrongdoing, and took responsibility for his actions. The others influenced him, but they did not own their part of the result. I told them that a value of our school community is that people not be bystanders to hurtful or prejudicial behaviors without speaking up or taking some other action. Bystanders who don't object are as responsible for the hurts to victims as are the original perpetrators, I believe. This is a value that some parents were not prepared to embrace.

I called the boys' parents to let them know about the incident. I told each of them that I knew their sons and that I didn't believe any of them would have behaved individually as they had when they were together that day at recess. Then I told them of my decision to give each of the children a half-day, in-house suspension and loss of recess for a week.

Some parents supported my decision. Others accepted it, but some of the parents were furious. How could I punish their child, who had not committed the act, to the same degree that I punished the one who had? They spoke heatedly with me and later with each other about the unfairness of my decision. In fact, it became quite the topic of conversation for a couple of days, and their anger was reignited as they spoke with one another.

In a meeting with the staff, I told them what had happened and what I had decided. Staff were being approached by parents, and I wanted them to know the full story before they responded. The teachers and noon aides supported my position, both with students and with parents. In fact, some publicly vocalized their support of my decision. We were all troubled that some parents were unwilling to let their children take, or learn to take, responsibility for their actions.

One parent approached me in the hallway a couple of days later. She said that she had heard about the incident the night before from several disgruntled parents. "I told them that I agreed with your position. Someday our daughters will be with these boys in a bar or on dates. We will be very glad to know that these boys learned about not getting swept up in a group mentality that gets them to do things they've been taught not to do. We will want the boys to have learned from this lesson when they are out with our daughters." This parent understood precisely why I felt so strongly that I needed to respond quickly and firmly to the boys about the seriousness of betraying their own values because of a group dynamic.

Later that day, I was given pause when I heard from Patrick's mother. She explained that she and her husband had been totally prepared to support what I had done, but when they spoke with Patrick, they learned that he had removed himself from the other boys when he couldn't get them to stop what they were doing. She didn't think Patrick should be treated the same as the other boys, because he had chosen a different action. By walking away, Patrick had made his own statement about the wrongness of their actions. After all, she reasoned, it would have been asking a great deal to expect a 9-year-old to go get an adult when his friends were behaving poorly, even though that might be our hope.

Now I had a lot to think about. Because there were other parents who felt strongly that the boys' punishment was too harsh, if I changed my decision for Patrick, they would surely expect me to reverse it for their sons too. Yet what Patrick's mother said to me made sense. I consulted with a couple of colleagues and they agreed with me that I should modify Patrick's punishment in recognition of his behavior. I knew that I had to consider what was in his best interest, even if it meant that there might be a backlash from other parents. I met with Patrick, told him I had reconsidered, and rescinded his in-house suspension. He readily agreed to miss the recesses. I apologized for my initial judgment and told Patrick I was wrong. I told him I was influenced greatly by his mother's call, because she helped me to see that he had taken a stand and had not been a willing bystander to the situation.

During the boys' in-house suspensions, I spoke with each of them privately. I said that I knew what kind of people they were and was sure that this would not have happened had they been alone. I emphasized my concern that the group had greater power at the moment of the incident than each of them had exercised individually and that I wanted them to learn now, in a safe place, how to handle themselves in the future. I concluded with each boy by saying that I felt certain that he would learn from this and not be as likely to act out of pressure from a group in the future. Each one signaled to me, in his own way, that he understood what I was talking about. The boys were actually more accepting of my reaction than some of their parents had been.

The students knew that I valued them very much. It was their behavior at the moment that outraged me. My confidence in their future behavior reassured them and I made sure to signal to each of them several times over the next week that what had happened was over and I still cared about them. There would be no grudges on my part nor, I believed, on theirs.

I worked hard to reestablish good relationships with some of their parents, who remained critical of my decision. In fact, I never did hear from the other parents about my reversal of Patrick's punishment. Perhaps the other boys knew that it was fair and didn't tell their parents. They weren't hoping for a change in their consequences. Children usually have a strong sense of fairness. I respected the boys for how they handled their own punishments.

If we ask children to take a stand, and expect other adults to do it, we must be prepared to do it as well. Part of being a leader is being willing to act on what we believe even if we are initially uncomfortable doing so. As leaders, we must model this behavior.

It matters to me that we created a school community where people were accepted and protected. Although we may criticize or even punish someone for specific behaviors, we must not condemn the person. Not only do we not want to treat individuals that way, but we also need to remember to focus on what's best for the whole school community. People must know that they belong just because they exist, not because of accomplishments or missteps. They need to be certain that disagreements or misbehaviors may bring some specific consequence but will not jeopardize their sense of belonging in the school community.

TELLING OUR TRUTHS

Every year I sent out a letter to all the adults in our school community. I wrote the letter at the end of August, sharing my reflections on the connection between something I did during the summer and learning. I mailed the letter to the staff about a week before school began and put it in the "first day of school" packet for families. It was my way of welcoming people back to school and sharing a little about myself.

I never knew how most people reacted to my letters, because they didn't tell me. I imagined that some people glanced at my letter and others may have thrown it away if they hadn't found them interesting in the past. Others may have read it out of personal curiosity but were less interested in the connections I made between my experiences and education. Some may have been annoyed that I sent it at all. I am aware of these possibilities, yet I wrote it each year because I hoped that there would be some for whom it was a welcome invitation to a new school year.

My letters were personal and informal. They were not the "It's September, let's get out the apples" type of communication. They were different. That was intentional. Sending those letters at all was a bit unusual, but it felt important to me, and I worked to write something worth reading. One year, this is what I wrote:

> After putting on my swimsuit and critically eyeing my reflection in our bedroom mirror at Squam Lake, I went to the dock for a swim. I headed out and found myself swimming very close to two loons in our cove. Loons don't usually stay that close to people, so I was amazed that they continued their search for food so near to me. After each of them put its head underwater in search of food, it would then make a sound very different than its usual haunting wail. The previous night, Henry and I listened to that sound and wondered what they were communicating. Today Henry called out to me that the sound must be a compliment, and I was touched by his sweetness. The loons and I swam together a little longer, and then they went their way and I went mine.
>
> Thomson's beach was my goal, but when I got there I felt so good that I kept on going. I was enjoying my solitary swim, feeling the warmth of the sun on my face. My stroke was propelling me through the water and I glided past the trees along the shore. Becoming so attuned with the natural environment, I was momentarily stunned by a Squam Lake tour boat approaching me. Though I felt annoyed by the intrusion, I waved at the people in the boat

and smiled more broadly when the tour guide told me that they had thought I was a mermaid.

Perhaps this 46-year-old body wasn't as worthy of my self-criticism as I had thought. At least my husband and the gray-haired tour guide didn't think so, having just found two unique ways to convey their approval. As I swam, the word "acceptance" came to mind, and I mentally repeated it in time with my strokes. Acceptance, acceptance, I thought as I glided through the water and felt more and more content. I felt peaceful and strong, continuing to swim much farther than I had ever gone before.

"Maybe I'll swim to that rock," I thought, as I moved through the lake, keeping pace with the movement of the clouds overhead. "I'm already there; I think I'll keep on going." The more I thought about acceptance, the further I swam. I made it all the way to Little Heron Cove! I couldn't believe it.

Reflecting on my experience, I realized that I was energized by the feeling of acceptance and actually able to do more because of the freedom. I want to remember this awareness because I believe it will help me, and perhaps others, to come closer to reaching our potential in ways that feel congruent with our essence.

Sincerely,

Susan Villani

I knew my letter that year was more unusual because I mentioned my critical reaction to seeing my image when I wore my bathing suit. Sharing such a personal response is not what principals typically discuss. Yet with all the concern we have as a society about being thin and beautiful, it didn't seem too outrageous to acknowledge that I am also susceptible to those pressures. Although my feelings of self-acceptance initially were triggered by comments from my husband and the tour guide, I hoped what I learned from my experience would enable me to prompt myself to be more self-accepting in the future.

There was more feedback than usual to my letter that year. Some staff members remarked that they enjoyed it and thought about what I wrote. A few parents were very enthusiastic about it after they received it on the first day of school. One mother told me that she was so impressed by my letter that she read it to her son, discussing it with him afterward.

"I loved your letter!" one father called out to me as I was driving through the center of town. I noticed that I was surprised to hear that comment from a man, catching myself in the assumption that it would be women who would relate more strongly to a message about self-acceptance, particularly because it involved "body acceptance."

Then I got a call from the superintendent of schools asking me whether I had heard about Sally's letter to him and the school committee. Sally was a parent who was very active in the school and district. I braced myself for I knew not what and replied, "No, I haven't. What does it say?"

"She's ripping your letter," was the gist of his response.

I was flabbergasted. "What does she say is wrong with it?" The superintendent couldn't tell me, because Sally had not been specific.

I asked the superintendent whether he would like a copy of the letter to see whether he thought it was objectionable. He said that she had attached a copy of my letter to her own, so he had already seen it. "Susan, you have to admit it is a little unusual."

"Sure it is," I answered, "but so what? I have done other things that are unusual and they have benefited the school. I send a personal letter at the end of every summer. Do you see anything in particular that would be so offensive to a parent in this one?" He didn't, and said that he had discussed it with a school committee member, who noted its uniqueness, but also didn't understand what was such a problem.

The superintendent suggested that I call Sally and ask her, which is exactly what I had intended to do. Sally and I had worked together on many school-related projects. I knew her to be an intelligent and articulate person who stood behind what she believes. When I reached her, I said that I heard she was offended by my letter and was calling to find out what it was that she found objectionable.

You could have knocked me over with a feather when I heard Sally's response. It was something like, "Oh Susan. Come on. Essence? Your essence? If someone gets a hold of this letter and reads it at town meeting, there won't be any way that we can defend the school budget to the community with a principal writing a letter like this."

I thought for a moment. Even if I had done something outrageous, which I hadn't, I couldn't believe that the townspeople would refuse to pass the school budget. They might look to the superintendent to address my performance, but they wouldn't take out their frustrations on all the children in town. It was clear to me that Sally was attributing far more weight to my letter than was warranted.

I told her that I was sorry that she felt that way and that I would think about it. I reread the letter, trying to see things from her perspective. "Essence." "Congruent with our essence." I didn't get it. That seemed fairly innocuous to me. It was another way of saying "true to ourselves." As I thought about it more, I wondered whether it was really the word "essence" that bothered her, or rather its context: the principal looking at her body in the mirror and then swimming and thinking about self-acceptance.

I heard more about the letter each day. I showed it to a few people I respected and asked for their responses. They too were puzzled by the intensity of the feedback I got from Sally. I was disappointed that she hadn't told me her concerns before speaking to the superintendent and the school committee. I realized that she probably did represent a segment of readers who didn't like the letter. Receiving positive feedback about my letter from parents, almost daily, validated that some found value in what I had shared.

My response to this event was different from what it had been to other criticisms in the past. This time, I didn't see anything wrong with what I had done, and if I had it to do over again, I would act the same. I wouldn't refrain from writing and sending the letter, and I didn't feel scared or sorry. I actually felt empowered by my self-assurance on this issue.

If talking about self-acceptance is so disturbing, then I think we have a lot of work ahead of us. Girls as young as 8 years old are succumbing to anorexia and bulimia, teens are committing suicide at alarming rates, and many people abuse alcohol and drugs, in part because they are not comfortable with themselves. We had better start talking more about self-acceptance. In fact, the amount and intensity of people's reactions to my letter confirmed that I had touched on something people needed to think about.

HOW WE ARE KNOWN

In the summer letter, I had chosen to tell a story about myself, sharing my thoughts and feelings about an issue I considered relevant to a school community. Even if the feedback had been largely negative, I would not have regretted writing my letter. In healthy organizations and communities, disagreement is part of constructive communication and growth. I welcomed people's reactions and feelings about all aspects of my leadership and the school, but I drew the line at being told I should not say what I thought because it was controversial. As I saw it, raising important issues was part of being a conscientious principal. It was not my job to take the safe path.

A principal must be ready, I believe, to influence a school community about educational issues. If there are too many people who don't want for their children what the principal strives to provide, then the principal may no longer be as effective.

I must admit that there were times when I wondered whether the extra tasks I initiated were worth the time and effort. Sending out the summer letters was an additional job to do at a busy time. Yet each time I considered abandoning them, I remembered that I had established a tradition of summer letters. Many in our school community had told me that they looked forward to receiving them.

My role, as I saw it, was to promote thinking, among adults as well as children. I felt proud that the staff and I sustained an environment that was perceived as welcoming and friendly, where children felt safe to learn. We had worked to make sure that differences were acceptable, and in so doing it became safe for each of us—students, teachers, staff, and administrator—to be ourselves.

As educators and parents, we know the importance of modeling for children. To be comfortable as role models, we must be accepting of ourselves and confident about what we have to offer. Parents and teachers are daily models for children. As a school principal, I was in a position to be a model as a learner, leader, a woman, a risk taker, and someone who was comfortable having feelings and sharing them.

When children shared their perceptions of me, I saw which messages came through to them. Adrian, a 3rd-grader, once came to my office to tell me about a poetry anthology done at his previous school and that he wanted our school to consider producing one. I agreed that it was a interesting idea and suggested he speak with the language arts specialist. He continued telling me about the anthology and why it would be good for our school. After several attempts to get him to speak with the person who might act on his suggestion, I said, "You don't seem to want to speak with her. Why not?"

Figure 3.2   "Women Can Be Good Principals" poster. Created by and reproduced with permission of Jennifer L. Nardone.

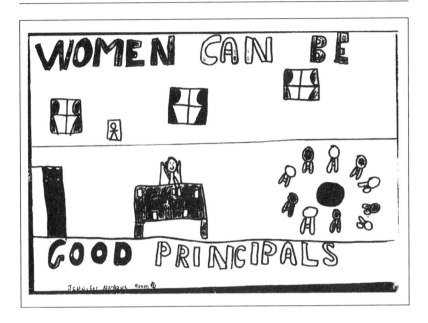

Adrian smiled patiently at me and explained, "When I told you that I speak another language and that my picture should be included on the ESL display, it happened. I figure you are the person to talk to if I want to see something get done." Clearly, for this student I was a principal who acted on ideas.

Another student expressed her belief that "women can be good principals" in the caption of a poster she created for a career exploration program at the school. In it, my office was pictured, including the chairs arranged on the braided rug, ready for student dialogue. For this student, the principal was approachable and helped students solve problems together.

When your actions reflect your philosophy, you are modeling what you hope children will do. There are additional steps you can take to concretize their perceptions. The following are examples of my efforts to do so.

After I earned my doctorate in educational administration, I decided to use the title "doctor" in school. I wanted the students to become as accustomed to calling a woman "doctor" as they would be to calling a man "doctor." I just had to make sure that they didn't think I was going to give them painful injections or bad-tasting medicine. I wanted them to understand how much studying is required to be a principal, and what an important job it is to be the leader of a school.

Each year I include something in my weekly schedule that involved learning something new. One year it was taking flute lessons with some 5th-graders and being a member of our school band. Another year I was an art student with the same class for an entire school year, facing the same challenges and feeling the same satisfaction when my work resulted in a product I was proud to see displayed. I think it's important for students to see adults in situations that greatly challenge them and for adults to be able to share their frustration as well as their elation.

Every year in one school, we took the 5th-grade students away for a three-day outdoor education experience. When I climbed 60 feet up a tree and walked across a cable on the high ropes course, students saw me as a learner and risk taker—in the same position they were in. That year I was so frightened by being so high in the air that when I came down, I started crying.

"Why are you crying, Dr. Villani? You did it and you're down now."

I replied, "Because it was very scary and my mind hasn't caught up with my body. But it sure felt great to do it." I was experiencing several emotions simultaneously: fear, pride, and exhilaration. I wanted students to see that we all have those feelings and that it is all right to show them.

I also wanted to be a role model for students about writing. I think that the written word is very powerful. The summer letters I wrote sometimes elicited strong reactions from people. Many told me that they related to the feelings I described or that they thought a lot about what I wrote. So the letters were a good example of using words to express an experience, a feeling, or a strong opinion about another's writing. When Sally wrote about my summer letter, she emphasized the power of writing, both as a reader and a responder. She may have modeled for her own children the importance of being able to express oneself so clearly and emphatically. It is imperative that our students learn how to think and be able to express their ideas through their writing, as well as through their speaking and actions.

Each year, right before the end of school, I gave students a pen with an inscription about satisfaction in knowing they gave their very best at school and at home. I went to every class to hand out my small gifts to the children. "I think writing is very important," I told them one year. "I hope that these pens will remind you to keep writing during the summer. Write a letter or a postcard, write in your journal, write a poem, write a shopping list if you need one, but keep writing." The children laughed when I got to the part about the shopping list, and I knew that they understood my point.

If the students heard that a letter I wrote elicited powerful reactions (and we know that children do hear things that their parents whisper to keep from their ears), they saw a real-life illustration that the written word is a very powerful tool. Even if the children knew nothing about the substance of the letter, they will have known that I followed my own advice to them and wrote during the summer. Maybe in the future when they have a strong feeling, they will write a letter, a poem, a book, or an editorial and share it.

ACCEPTING OURSELVES

When I think back to the young woman, newly appointed, who worked so hard to look like a principal by wearing gray, brown, or blue suits, I see how much difference 21 years made. I have come to know more about who I am on the inside and I feel freer to be authentic on the outside. Deciding to wear a pink blazer on a television program or wearing floral dresses in addition to suits were beginning ways I chose to share myself without apology. Other, more important ways emerged.

In the later years of my principalship, no one called me "the new little girl." I noticed that I was, after all those years, more comfortable letting my emotions show in my facial expressions. Once, while interviewing a candidate for a teaching position, she revealed that the death of her two brothers greatly affected her desire to become a teacher. My eyes filled with tears as she spoke. When she noticed my reaction, she stopped talking. She hadn't anticipated anything like that happening in an interview.

I told her that I was deeply moved by her story. When she saw that I was comfortable with my spontaneous reaction, she continued. She later wrote to thank me for the interview, and commented, "You are the first person who has interviewed me that responded so strongly to what I said about my family. You must be a very sensitive principal, and I would love to work in your school."

I had become comfortable with the fact that I am a passionate person who laughs and cries easily. I believe that my passion enhanced my effectiveness much of the time. People saw that sharing more of myself came from a deep belief that being authentic is necessary in a professional learning community. When I left my last principalship, an administrator wrote: "Thanks for being the one to ensure that a very authentic, human perspective *always had a champion at the Administrative Council meetings over these past years.*"

As people worked with me or observed me as a principal, the reactions were, of course, mixed. With some, I earned trust by being more real, more human, and more open, and they were encouraged to risk being more authentic themselves. There have been times, however, when sharing my feelings of sadness or vulnerability fueled some people's inclination to slander me. There have been several individuals who, when they thought they perceived weakness, saw an opportunity for attack. It has been my experience that while others may initially be influenced by such attacks, in the long run they realized the deception and thought less of those who had chosen that course of action.

It takes courage to be authentic. Sharing one's thinking and feelings while they are happening is much more difficult, because the context keeps changing and the outcomes are unpredictable. For me, deciding to take risks depends on what I think might be gained and what might be lost.

I believe that aspects of authentic leadership are subtler than other leadership behaviors, and they may require a longer time to understand. Focusing on process and relationship takes more time than decision making from above, and the staff initially may have viewed me as being less decisive and less able to achieve results. As we worked together and as I clarified my approach, many people understood my leadership and trusted it.

Even when I hadn't made the conscious choice to reveal some part of myself, some people—often children—saw it anyway. One day, when I was observing an art teacher, a 1st-grader approached me.

He asked, "Are you Dr. Villani? You look a little different."

I had just gotten a haircut, and I asked whether he thought that might be it.

"Yeah, but you also look different in your face," Charlie replied.

"What looks different in my face?" I wondered.

"It looks a little more wrinkly."

You might think I would have felt very deflated or angry about what Charlie said, but those weren't my reactions. I was curious. I said, "When you wave to me from the hall and I'm sitting at my desk, you're farther away from me. Maybe you're closer to me now and can see the wrinkles better."

Charlie backed up to approximate the distance at which he usually sees me, peered at me for a while, with his thumb and fore-finger framing his chin, and then concluded that I definitely had more wrinkles than when he saw me last week.

"Do you think I got these wrinkles during one week?" I asked.

"Maybe during the weekend."

I had indeed had a very troubling weekend, and what this little guy had observed was probably the tension I still carried in my face. Charlie's perceptiveness astounded me. Sometimes I was unintentionally transparent.

If an adult had made a similar statement, I would have won-dered whether criticism and judgment were implied. Charlie, though, was merely reporting what he observed, as casually as he would describe any detail he noticed. It felt good to be seen with-out being judged.

A sign in that art room proclaimed "Be yourself. Accept others." Charlie had given me an object lesson for which I was grateful. In the day-to-day functioning of a school, leaders spend nearly all their time supporting and facilitating the growth of the children and the adults in that community. It is imperative that we also reflect on ourselves and our own practice. In so doing, we may make stronger contributions to our learning communities and affect the ability of others to do more of the same.

CHAPTER FOUR

Building Community

In recognition of all the advice, aid, help, assistance, hand-holding, lesson plans, materials, humor, goodwill, mentoring, butt-covering, chicken soup, advocacy, support, flowers, gifts, smiles, rescuing, collegiality, direction, camaraderie, confidence, and friendship, we, the second-year teachers, thank you!

(Certificate of Appreciation presented to the
faculty by second-year teachers, fall 1996,
Thoreau School, Concord, MA)

It is important to acknowledge that not all members of the school community are represented through stories in this chapter. I have the deepest respect for the contributions of the support staff I worked with in each school, including the secretaries, nurses, custodians, paraprofessionals, and technology staff, as well as the parents, families, and larger community of the town. No school functions well without their commitment to the growth of the students and adults in the school community, and it is often their work behind the scenes that makes the rest of the staff look good.

MAKING ALL STUDENTS
FEEL PART OF THE COMMUNITY

I invited parents to bring their children in to meet me as soon as they knew they would be attending the school. We sat in my office and I acknowledged some of the things they might think about as new students in our school. "What are the kids like? Will I have any friends? Where's the bathroom? What will my teacher be like? Is the work hard?"

I told them, "I want to be one of your first friends to start with. If you have a problem, besides your teacher and the nurse and the social worker, I also would be happy to listen. Maybe I could help. I like to hear good news, too, and if you ever want to give me some art or writing you've done, I love to decorate my office with student work."

After answering any questions they had, we went on a tour of the building. As we walked, I was able to begin to get to know them. Because we already had covered the pressing questions, we chatted as we walked, and their personalities were more visible as they became more relaxed.

I brought them into the class they would be in and introduced them to their teacher and students. Then, with my hand on their shoulder, I said to the class, "How would you feel if you were coming to a new school and the principal just started giving you a tour of the building? She's got her hand on your shoulder and you're wondering what she's going to do or say next. How would you feel if you didn't know the teachers, the kids, or if there was going to be recess? Well, I don't know for sure, but maybe Les is feeling some of these things. Who can tell Les something about our school?"

The children said they liked recess, the teachers are really nice, and we have special events like the "Turkey Trot" and the "Lip Sync." Then I asked, "Would you please raise your hand if you'll be a buddy for Les? Who will show him (or her) around when he (or she) gets here. Who will eat lunch with him (or her)?" Many hands were quickly raised and the tension in the new student's shoulders started to dissipate. Within 10 minutes, the new pupils had more offers of friendship than they knew what to do with. As we walked back to my office, they were usually much more relaxed.

Knowing what to anticipate goes a long way toward reducing anxiety about being new to a school. After that, the new students could focus on the school with anticipation rather than fear. It usually went very well after that because the teachers took over, and they were masters at helping kids join their classroom communities.

ACCEPTANCE BASED ON BEING

I believe that what informs the practice of many teachers and administrators is their experiences at home and in school as learners. Although we continue to learn about our profession by studying educational theories and collaborating with colleagues, formative childhood experiences often ground our beliefs.

I'm sure that I paid particular attention to students' entry to school because of some of my feelings of insecurity when I was a youngster, and even because of my confusion about what being a youngster meant. As a capable and perceptive child, I was noted for accomplishments and behavior seemingly beyond my years. My parents seemed so delighted with my achievements that I wanted to keep bettering my last accomplishment, and I aspired to act older because I thought it was more desirable.

High-achieving students often receive a lot of attention for their accomplishments. They may think that their acceptance is based on their performance and feel compelled to repeat or top their accomplishment to continue being accepted. I, too, confused competence with acceptance and, furthermore, based my self-acceptance on the approval or admiration of others.

I remember, as a young girl, wanting to wear my skirts at knee length like my mother and refusing to wear them as short as other little girls my age. I wouldn't accept lollipops at the doctor's office and refused to go on the rides at the amusement park. My parents took my brother and me there to enjoy ourselves, but I hated going. It wasn't clear to me then, but in retrospect I think I found it confusing to be at a park where I was expected to act like a child, when at other times I was praised for being adultlike. But for all my yearning to be seen as mature, I surely had the developmental needs of any child my age to feel safe and accepted.

I took this wish to achieve and be recognized further than my parents wished. There was the time when my mother offered me the treat of my choice—my first lipstick—if I would just do something that came naturally to most kids. What was so difficult for me to do that she felt she needed to bribe me to do it? To go outside and play after school, and not spend every afternoon redoing homework until it was perfect. My father even offered to institute payment for my report card if I received B's instead of A's. It was obvious to my parents that my concern about doing things perfectly was not serving me well. They clearly wanted me to have more balance in my days and more childlike experiences.

My teacher also expressed concern about me. She knew about the bargain my mother had made with me and proposed something new to me as well. She wanted me to work on homework for only an hour each day, and promised that she wouldn't punish me if I didn't finish everything. The day after we made this arrangement, the teacher was reviewing the spelling words with the class. When she called on me to say whether I would wear a b-o-w or a b-e-a-u in my hair, and I said a b-e-a-u, she replied, "That would be awfully large to put in your hair!" The whole class's laughter stung more than a swarm of bees, and though everyone else probably forgot it in moments, for me it throbbed for quite a long time.

Like the other students who had been recalcitrant about learning their spelling words, I had to stay in from recess to learn them. I was not accustomed to being in the group of those who did not do what they were supposed to do. I vowed never again to let myself get in that predicament because of incomplete assignments. What was a throwaway comment by my teacher, which she never intended as hurtful, annihilated my ability to trust her, especially because she had been the one to initiate the bargain about limiting study time. I had tried to do what my teacher proposed, and it resulted in my getting even less of the acceptance and approval I sought.

I wanted to be a doer, like my father, so the focus of my learning became the acquisition of skills. He liked to help my brother and me learn new things, gain confidence in our ability, and participate with others in some of the activities that had not been available to him when he was a child.

One winter we each got our first pair of ice skates. We bundled up and went down to the lake. My father put on his ice skates first and figured out how to use them. Brooklyn born and raised, he had never ice-skated, but after about 15 minutes he felt confident enough to bring us out on the ice to teach us.

My father was a professional saxophonist, and music had been an important part of his life since he was a teenager. He organized a band with my brother, my cousins, and me, and after several rehearsals we performed our signature song, "Volare," at the school talent show. My father's delight in our performance underscored my connection with him through music. I enjoyed our closeness at these times and I realized that my achievement in playing the piano resulted in a very satisfying link with my father.

My father's reaction to my fears about any form of inadequate performance was to help me do better. When I was afraid that I would strike out in softball games at school, my father responded by spending hours pitching to me so that I could become a competent batter. I came to believe that my intelligence and willingness to work hard would be the keys to my success. Although learning skills in many arenas is very important, I needed to develop a sense of self-worth and purpose that would always be with me, even when I couldn't be especially skillful or solve problems by working hard.

Learning that we may be accepted because of who we are, not because of what we do, was a lesson a long time in coming for me. I think it was when I started teaching 1st grade and had those feelings of acceptance for each of my students that I began to rethink my childhood belief that acceptance had to be earned by high achievement. I realized that I cared about my students, not because of what they achieved, but just because. Because I felt that way about them, it dawned on me that others, especially my parents, had felt that way about me. I wish I had been able to see that at the time. Making sure students saw it became a major focus of my teaching and leading.

HIRING NEW TEACHERS AND PROMOTING TEACHER DEVELOPMENT

Bringing talented, creative, collaborative, and diverse risk-takers into a school to join existing talented staff is one of the most important things a principal or an administrative team does. Parents are sometimes skeptical of new teachers, fearing their inexperience will mean they are insufficiently knowledgeable or skillful. Parents may be concerned about whether new staff members share their values. When I earned a reputation for hiring exceptional teachers, it helped parents trust that the new teachers would be positive additions to our school and good for their children.

I recall one year in which staffing was particularly challenging. After a retirement, a leave of absence, a voluntary transfer, and an increase in enrollment, I was in the enviable position of being able to hire five teachers. Some of my administrator colleagues felt sorry for me because each new hire required five formal observations and write-ups and an evaluative summary. They feared the paperwork might do me in. I said that I would rather go down that way, if it came to it, than not have the opportunity to bring in exciting and talented teachers.

I interviewed more than 75 people for those positions, after screening countless resumes and conferring with the director of personnel. It was very time-consuming, yet it was worth every minute. I met incredible people and recommended we hire a most diverse group of men and women of different ages and ethnicities. I believe it is important for children to see school staff who look like them or share their traditions. This would mean we needed to hire people of their race, ethnicity, or religion. Because teachers are often role models for children, it is imperative that the faculty be diverse. We were hiring talented teachers who would bring new perspectives and capabilities to the entire school community, not just their own classrooms.

A newly hired music teacher shared her talent with our entire school community, while making a strong statement about the values of our school, when she wrote our school song. She conferred with colleagues to get ideas about the type of music that would be most welcomed, as well as lyrics that would be meaningful for the children and the adults in our school. Her creation was a triumph. We proudly sang it at school events. The music and words reinforced our beliefs, our sense of belonging, and our commitment to each other.

I didn't want divisions among the staff I hired and their incumbent colleagues. I made sure to speak about the contribution new members could make to an already strong and experienced staff. To my relief, veteran staff readily accepted these people, realizing their value and respecting them. Parents carefully watched these new teachers as well and made their own assessments. The teachers were excellent, and my reputation for hiring went up a notch.

After that year, teachers that I recommended for hire had the advantage of positive anticipation by many parents, who, for the

Figure 4.1   The Thoreau School Song. Composed by Susan Tuttle.

most part, strongly approved of the people hired since I came. When a school community anticipates that new staff will strengthen the school and be good for the children, it makes an enormous difference in the likelihood of success for the people hired. As teachers new to the school became oriented to working in a new environment, they were given the benefit of time to show what they could do, rather than being judged on their teaching the minute they walked in the door. Just as children need to feel safe to learn, adults are able to perform their best when they feel safe.

WHAT WE HAVE IN COMMON

A sense of community that also embraces individuality takes time to build. When I first became a principal, I was not aware of how gradual and deliberate the building process would need to be.

That first year, when it came time to do evaluations of teachers, I created evaluation packets and distributed them to all the teachers. I asked the teachers to write their "philosophy of education" and "growth plans" for the coming year, as had once been done by a principal when I was a teacher. My intent was to acknowledge that it wouldn't be fair for me to walk into classrooms and make judgments about performance without first ascertaining what the teachers were trying to do. I wanted to show my support of their own goal-setting and believed that this would be an appropriately respectful process for evaluating teachers.

I wanted to offer something to an experienced staff, many of whom had been teachers far longer than I. I envisioned the evaluation packet as an opportunity for self-reflection and dialogue and hoped that could be one of my contributions. As it happened, the teachers nearly had a fit when they read what I had written, and although I heard their responses, I couldn't believe my ears.

"Growth plan! Philosophy of education! What does she think we're doing here?"

"I don't have time to sit around and write all this stuff."

"She's the principal. Let her come in and evaluate me. That's her job. It's not my job to write a thesis for her!"

My efforts to explain my thinking or clarify my intentions did not help. Yet I firmly believed that to walk in "cold" and make judgments would be a setup for all of us. If I was judging performance based on criteria we hadn't discussed, how likely would they be to meet my expectations? How would I know what they, in turn, hoped I would see and comment on?

I insisted that people try my process and that we would see how it worked. I hoped that the teachers would see that it wasn't a trick, but rather an earnest attempt to promote dialogue about what they were doing and why. But my attempts to engage people mostly resulted in stony silence or begrudging answers that revealed as little as possible about themselves. No one seemed interested in discussing teaching methodology or philosophy. After a while I felt defeated and just wanted to get the evaluations done. "Maybe another year will be better, after people see that I'm not out to get them," I told myself.

In retrospect, I think that the teachers may have feared being evaluated on what they wrote as their philosophy and growth plan. I think they felt that the evaluation itself would begin the minute they put pen to paper, even though my intention had been to use the growth plan as a way for them to express their individuality, their challenges, and their goals. The evaluation of their performance would come after. If I had realized that a fear or reluctance to write was the issue, I could have had a conversation with each teacher in advance of my observation. Our discussions could have achieved what I wanted and might have felt less onerous to the teachers. Unfortunately, they did not trust my intention and I was bewildered by their responses.

Ironically, it was something totally unrelated that helped us build relationships. I got married. You may wonder what this has to do with anything. So did I.

When the teachers found out that I was planning to get married, they had a shower for me, and their warmth surprised me even more than the event itself did. I started to realize that by getting married I was choosing to do something that most of them also had done. We would now have something in common.

Years later, at a faculty meeting, I shared with the teachers a poem I had written, and it created quite a stir:

I have a new growth plan of which you should know.

It's something quite special, and beginning to show.

As with a good growth plan, a goal is the start,

And ways to achieve it, these come from the heart.

This plan involved people; it's not achieved alone.

The involvement of another has already shown.

It will mean temporary changes in our school and how it's run.

I need your help and ideas so that it's satisfactorily done.

Our work is education, and for that we need the student.

With enrollments so declining, I'm doing what is prudent—

I'm growing one!

When the teachers realized I was pregnant, they talked with me about their experiences being pregnant. They offered suggestions and advice. There was another shower, this time for the baby. I cherished the cradle they had commissioned a colleague's husband to build.

What I had not been able to do through the language of growth plans and goal statements was happening in other ways. We were growing closer as we realized that there were things that were similar about us, in addition to the obvious differences. I could feel their skepticism melting away. We were learning to trust each other.

I'm not recommending getting pregnant as the solution to poor relationships with the staff. That would be a bit extreme. Yet I learned a powerful lesson about the many unexpected ways there may be to achieve the goal of building relationships with staff.

I had not considered the importance of how different I seemed to the staff when I first became principal. The teachers had gotten stuck in thinking about the ways that we were different, and they focused on trying to keep their school as it was before I arrived. I was focused on our working together for the good of the students and had given much less consideration to finding ways to build bridges so the staff and I could come together. I now better understand how talking about sports or food may help build relationships and eventually serve larger organizational goals. They are ways that some people make connections. Those connections may then be the foundation upon which people build trust so that they are ready to collaborate on educational goals.

The benefit of having been a principal for so many years is that I can now understand what was not evident to me at the beginning of my career—what would have helped us connect more quickly. As important as it was for me to establish myself in ways that were congruent with my beliefs, it was crucial that I discover ways to connect and build relationships with the people with whom I wanted to work.

LONELY AT THE TOP

Finding commonalities can help principals connect with their staff, and these connections are often solidified when there is a threat from outside the group. A new principal may be viewed as the outsider. I remember such a situation from my second year as a teacher. The principal had been newly appointed and was about to discover how the existing faculty would become unified through their opposition to a new leader.

There was a specialist in this school whom teachers reported had very little control of the classes she taught. Although she was dedicated to her specialty, the students did not follow her instructions, sometimes running around the classrooms and even standing on desks. Teachers complained to the principal. Finally, in the spring, word got out that the principal had recommended that the teacher not be rehired. Suddenly everyone was outraged by his action, and a petition was circulated among the teachers, stating to the principal that the teacher was outstanding and definitely an asset to the school.

I had just become a teacher the year before and wanted very much to feel solidarity with my colleagues. I was trying to learn from them what it meant to be a professional educator. Yet I had heard them bad-mouth the teacher, and now they were saying things that directly contradicted their own previous statements.

I felt that what was happening was wrong, but I was afraid to alienate my new colleagues. As it turned out, I didn't have to take a stand, because untenured teachers had not been asked to sign the petition, because of possible jeopardy to their job security. Nevertheless, I felt that I should speak up. The compromise that I worked out with myself was to speak privately with the principal. I told him about the petition he was about to receive and my discomfort with it. I explained my bewilderment about the whole situation and said that I felt guilty for not confronting my new colleagues. He appreciated my sentiments and told me that he didn't expect me to voice my concern to them.

Being in his first year as principal, he, too, was bewildered. He questioned the teachers' commitment when they changed their stories about this teacher's competence after he had taken the very action they had been suggesting all year. The superintendent and the school committee ultimately accepted the principal's recommendation, but the principal was very disheartened by the staff's response.

In my own principalships, I have had similar experiences in which teachers complained adamantly about a colleague's behavior, demanding I do something about it, and then disowned their role and opinions when others asked whether they knew what had prompted my actions. I learned to act only on what I saw or what people would be willing to acknowledge publicly if asked. I also realized how beneficial it was for me when people remembered what they had seen me do in the past and reconsidered the likelihood of whatever unfair actions were being attributed to me.

One teacher who sensed the frustration and pain I was experiencing about a difficult situation at school wrote me the following letter. It reflected the teacher's understanding of some of the dynamics of leadership.

> I came here because you are the leader for whom I want to work. You have always made it a point to show your support and recognition. I, too, hope you feel my support. . . . But superior leaders don't always win the endorsement of the majority. When perspectives aren't agreed upon, there is always a chance that people will misunderstand one another. What is important is that you stand behind your beliefs. I believe that you do that with diplomacy and grace.

Lee's words were a great comfort. I didn't expect Lee to do or say anything publicly. The letter indicated an awareness and validation that provided me with the private support I needed. I saved it as a reminder that even when staff were silent about an issue, they may have noticed and understood my intentions and actions.

SHARING LEADERSHIP: WHEN AND HOW

One day I was having lunch with a 1st-grader in my office. She was making conversation, asking me whether I had enjoyed the weekend, what was my favorite color, where did I live, and whether I had children. When she started to run out of questions, she asked, "How old are you?" When I told her that I was 42, she asked, "Oh God, how did that happen?" I've been asking myself that same question.

In the course of 21 years as a principal, I learned many things. As I matured in the role, I realized that joint problem solving, shared decision making, and teacher empowerment are crucial, and it is the principal's role to facilitate them while protecting the rights of all constituencies.

When leaders are clear with the staff and students' families about their roles in the mutual goal of promoting students' growth and achievement, energies are used constructively. A leader's responsibility to foster community includes attending to each constituency, both individually and as they interact with other constituencies. To be attuned to the members of a school community, leaders need to communicate effectively. In addition, leaders need to know themselves, share themselves, and carefully consider their relationships with students, families, and staff. The contributions and interactions of each of these constituencies are what make a school dynamic.

Class Placement: What's Best for Students?

One of the first things that parents in every school system discussed with me is how their children would be assigned to classroom teachers. Because parents care so much about their children, it is not surprising that many of them were very concerned that their children get "the best" teacher each year. Yet what does it mean to be the best, and how does one know who is the best teacher at each grade level? Is there really a "best"?

Parents formulate opinions about teachers in many ways. The experience of an older child in that teacher's class is one way; observations during chance encounters in school are another. Neighbors are a big source of information, and opinions about "the best" teachers are often shared.

As teachers develop reputations in the community, parents begin to refer to the teacher who is "good at self-esteem building" as if that description applies to only one person. It is sometimes amusing to hear different parents express the same needs for their children and then name different teachers as the only ones who can meet their needs. Obviously, many teachers can do what is requested, yet parents may know of only one of them by reputation or direct experience. I have worked hard to help people understand that there is not one "best" teacher; rather, there are teachers who have different skills that may serve students in different ways.

In addition to teacher–student matches, it is very important to consider the mix of students in each class, because peer interactions can greatly affect student behavior and achievement. A simple sign-up process for classes, as some parents have suggested, would not ensure the needed academic, physical, and social balance. Whereas specific teachers may be especially talented in certain ways, the children need to be equally divided into different classrooms because too many children of similar needs in one room will make it difficult for any teacher to serve the needs of all the children in the class. Parents don't have this information, and they usually have only their own child's needs in mind. The school, however, has a responsibility to meet the needs of all the children.

Although some parents were very trusting of what the school personnel did, others wanted to have a more active role in the process, wanting to pick their child's teacher or even select the peers with whom their child best related. I encouraged parent involvement, but placement cannot be decided solely on the basis of parents' preferences. It would not have been fair for the parents who were the most outspoken or who knew the principal the best to get what they wanted—and for the preferences of the rest of the parents to be ignored.

Through the years, I developed a placement process to ensure equal access. I mailed a letter to all families each March, outlining the placement process used at the school. It explained that a core placement team composed of individuals who had responsibilities

with children in all the grades of the school would make the placement decisions. Those people were the instructional specialists,
social worker, psychologist, speech and language therapists, and the
principal. In addition, the teachers of the sending grade level joined
the team to help place their students in the next grade's classes.

Parents were invited to fill out a form that indicated their view
of their child's strengths, challenges, and needs. In that way, they
could state what they thought worked well for their child in the
past and what they hoped for in the future. For many parents,
such a form was a comfortable vehicle for sharing their thoughts
with the school.

In my letter to families, I also included an invitation for them
to have a brief conference with me to share any special concerns.
As the letter explained, they could speak about what they were
experts in—their children. I told people that I didn't expect everyone to feel the need for such meetings, and that many very caring
and concerned parents did not meet with me.

When parents did wish to meet, I asked to hear their views on
what teaching methods and classroom protocol would be optimal
for their children. For example, some families had strong beliefs
about the value to students of readily observable structure and
discipline. They preferred a classroom in which the primary interactions are between the students and the teacher. They preferred
to see less movement around the room and less interaction among
the students during class time.

Other families looked closely to see whether the classroom had
opportunities for creative expression through a variety of media.
They liked to see students working together in small groups and
being animated and vocal in their interactions with each other.
All families wanted their children to learn. Their ideas about what
best promotes learning, however, were very different.

Many parents appreciated the invitation to speak directly with
me about their concerns. I made it clear to parents that the conference was a time to tell the principal what type of teacher and class
they wanted for their child, not which teacher or class they preferred. I discouraged parents from telling me which teacher they
thought best did what they wanted and should, therefore, be their
child's teacher the next year. Parents might be surprised to hear
how vulnerable teachers felt about conversations that parents had
about them during neighborhood sports practices and local events.
Because these conversations occurred in public settings, teachers

were concerned that they might be judged harshly by anyone present based on incomplete, if not erroneous, information. In my meetings, some parents tried to "work the system" by alluding to traits of a specific teacher that made their preferences clear, such as "My child is very creative, so he should have a teacher who does drama." Even without a name, if there was only one teacher at the grade level who put on student plays, the teacher's identity was clear. By insisting that parents follow the guidelines for parental input in the placement process, I hoped that teachers felt more assured that unfair judgments about them would not determine class placement.

Different assumptions about what influenced me were reflected in the ways people chose to approach me. If a father who was not usually involved in communication with the school about his child accompanied his wife to a placement conference and did all the talking, I sometimes speculated that his presence was intended to convey more authority or clout than hers alone. In those moments, I wondered whether what I've stood for and modeled about gender equity had been clear. Didn't they recognize my great respect for children's mothers? I felt disheartened by any assumption that a father's wishes or demands should count more than a mother's. I reminded myself that those parents were trying to do whatever they thought would work to their child's advantage. Being a parent myself, I could identify with parents' motivations even when I disagreed with the ways they acted on them.

I have never heard of another principal who routinely invited parents to meet to discuss placement. Some years I had as many as 100 such placement conferences, which took up the better part of several weeks and were emotionally taxing as well. Many of my administrator colleagues thought that the practice of inviting parents to conference with me was not merely time consuming, it was sheer lunacy—especially because I made it clear that I wouldn't promise to give parents the teacher they wanted for their child. The majority of parents seemed to appreciate the time it took me to meet with everyone who requested a conference, and they valued their inclusion. Nevertheless, because they didn't get to choose the teacher, some parents still felt shut out of the placement process no matter how much opportunity they had been given to share their thoughts about their child.

One year I was so exasperated that I said to the secretary, "If I ever offer to do this again, shoot me." The following year, as I was sending out the letters to parents about placement, including the offer to meet with me, she sheepishly asked me whether I remembered what I had said. Luckily, she was a pacifist.

In spite of the inevitable aggravation, I would much rather have put in the time proactively than hear from dissatisfied parents after the placement decisions had been made. The placement process greatly reduced the number of requests for changes, and some parents who had disagreed with the placement decisions later acknowledged that the placement team's decision was correct after all. Even with all the time invested and all the drama, I still believe the process served the students best.

Class Placement: What's Best for the Teacher?

Teachers often know very little about how their colleagues teach because they are usually in their own classrooms teaching. Teachers rarely observed each other, although I encouraged them to do so. As a result, they may have made judgments about one another's teaching from their interactions outside the classroom. They also may have been influenced by what former students and students' parents had told them. Despite the fact that teachers lacked full information about other teachers, it was very important for them to have input into future class placement for the students they currently taught.

At one school, during my first year there, I was bombarded with criticisms about a specific teacher. As soon as I arrived at that school, many parents made very disparaging remarks about her. Several went so far as to say that unless I gave them assurances that their children would not be placed in her classroom the following year, they would begin making arrangements to send them to private school in September.

Because I was new to the school, I didn't know whether their concerns were legitimate or the result of incorrect information or unfair conclusions. Without knowing the history, I was not in a position to take as firm a stand against the threats as I would have, had I felt certain the allegations were unsubstantiated. The teacher they spoke about was not of the ethnicity of the majority of teachers and families, and I even wondered whether there might be some racism in the parents' comments.

Either way, I didn't believe that the parents' insistence was information the entire staff should know about, so I changed the placement process to protect the teacher's privacy. Placement would be done, I decided, by a core team consisting of the social worker, language arts specialist, learning disabilities specialist, speech and language therapist, and principal. Sending teachers would write recommendations about placement that would be strongly considered, but those teachers would not sit with the placement team.

Some teachers felt very hurt that they were excluded from the process, and others were furious. At the time, I felt that I could not reveal my reason without creating curiosity about the identity of the teacher involved. Although I tried to allude subtly to the dangers of teachers picking classes for one another, many teachers concluded that I was devaluing their input.

It was a mess. By the time it was over, I had alienated just about everyone. To top it all off, the teacher I had worked so hard to protect wound up being angry with me about another matter, and she very adamantly told her colleagues that I had not supported her when she needed it! For many years afterward, that teacher dramatically shunned me and engaged people in the school district in diatribes about me. Her behavior was an embarrassment. I often regretted my changes in the placement process to protect her.

I know why I did it, however. It wasn't just for her. I did it because I believed that whenever someone is humiliated, it has a detrimental effect on everyone involved. People feel mixed emotions that are difficult to sort out. Most likely they will feel sorry for the person who has been embarrassed. They may be angry with the person whom they believe to be causing the situation or the person making it public. They may be worried that such a thing could happen to them. Sometimes it can be even more confusing for them when they actually see the other point of view but feel disloyal about anything other than full support for their colleague. Such situations always affect the morale of the group.

Neither the individual teacher identified by the parents nor her colleagues ever knew what motivated me to change the process. There were extenuating circumstances that I simply would not share with the group. Sometimes principals have to make difficult decisions that people just won't be able to understand. I've found it very painful when I've felt misunderstood and misjudged and I couldn't defend myself by explaining my rationale.

In retrospect, telling the staff in advance about the situation we faced, without identifying the teacher's grade level, would have helped them understand my motivation for seeking another way to do placement. I should have been transparent about my thinking rather than trying to handle it alone. Instead of feeling shut out, people then could have joined me in finding a better way.

Solving a Problem Together

The 1st-grade teachers in one school approached me because they didn't want to continue being scheduled for the first lunch period. Early lunch curtailed morning work time and made for a much longer afternoon, when the students' endurance was waning. Teachers also found that the youngsters weren't even hungry at their assigned lunchtime because their morning recess and snack had ended only an hour earlier.

I told the 1st-grade teachers that I was unwilling to change the lunch schedule on my own. I would be willing to put the issue on a faculty meeting agenda if they were ready to state their case. They were reluctant, and for a couple of years they lived with the schedule as it was, rather than addressing it at a meeting with their colleagues. The next time the 1st-grade teachers spoke with me about their dissatisfaction with the lunch schedule, they were prepared to address this issue with their colleagues.

Changing the lunch schedule would have ramifications for specialist schedules, including art, music, and physical education. All classroom teachers were very invested in having schedules that they perceived to be optimal for their students. I put discussion of the lunch schedule on the agenda for the upcoming faculty meeting. We all anticipated that it would be a heated discussion, and our prediction was correct.

One upper-grade teacher remarked early in the meeting, "Over my dead body will we have early lunch. It would mean changing our whole schedule."

"I hope it doesn't come to that, but we are going to discuss it," I replied, trying to inject a note of levity into the meeting, which was becoming very tense.

Evidently no one wanted first lunch, and it looked like we might come to blows—verbally, that is—about who would be the unlucky ones. The people who knew that I had been a 1st-grade teacher before becoming a principal probably would have bet that I would decide in favor of the needs of 1st-grade students. Yet

I respected the teachers' advocacy for their classes and sought a way to capitalize on their investments in their students' needs.

We tried and tried, but we couldn't figure out how to fit all our students into the cafeteria in any other configuration than three lunch periods. Some classes had to go to early lunch. Tess, a 1st-grade teacher, said that she would be willing to have children eat in her classroom rather than have to eat so early in the cafeteria. This was the first solution that didn't just focus on lunchtimes, but rather on where lunches could be eaten.

Louise adamantly objected to having children eat in the classroom because of potential spills on the carpet and food smells for the rest of the day. There was also the issue of how to supervise children during lunch if they ate in individual classrooms. The teachers' contract guaranteed a duty-free lunch to teachers, and we had only a few "noon aides" to supervise the children in the cafeteria. If the children went to separate classrooms, we wouldn't have enough people to go around, and there was no additional money for supervision in the budget. With classroom hygiene and the teachers' contract as objections, it again seemed that there were too many obstacles for us to solve this problem to everyone's satisfaction.

The problems being aired were administrative issues. I believed that we had to deal with whatever got in the way of doing what was in the best interests of the children. Not solving a problem that affected children's learning was not an option. We had to persevere.

"There must be something we can come up with," I said, more as a question in my mind than the definitive statement I appeared to be making. "It seems a shame for some of our students to be disadvantaged because of a scheduling problem." I let silence have its effect. "What else could we do?" I pleaded, searching for a solution that was elusive.

I was appealing to the dedicated impulses of the staff. They could see that I was open to considering any solution. It was a prime time for the faculty to take a risk, because we seemed very close to defeat otherwise.

"I'd be willing to eat lunch with my own students," offered Tess, desperate not to get stuck with first lunch again. Her comment marked another turning point in the meeting. By stepping outside another box, Tess enabled others to think more creatively and kept the problem-solving discussion alive.

There was heated debate about setting a precedent if a teacher supervised her or his own students in a classroom during lunchtime. There also were concerns about how Jamie, the custodian, would feel when children carried trays of food through the hallways and into their classrooms. We clearly weren't out of the woods yet.

Seth wondered aloud, "What if we found another place for the children to eat so that they wouldn't be in their classrooms? Would that work?" Here was another teacher's attempt to stretch our thinking to new places, both literally and figuratively. I was excited and intrigued by people's creative alternatives.

Rather than a "Yeah, but" response, I wanted to maintain the momentum and convey the spirit of, "Wow, how would we make that work?" I responded that we definitely could think of different eating places, as long as we could figure out how to provide adequate supervision. So the teachers wouldn't be inhibited by a contractual concern, I also reassured them that we could state in advance that anything we tried would not be binding for future contracts.

Before we knew what was happening, teachers started volunteering to take turns doing lunch duty, if only we could find a place. We talked about kids eating in the hallway, but that didn't seem safe. Then Jean asked, "What about the gym?"

There were no physical education classes scheduled from noon until 1:00, so that space was available. We identified the potential obstacles to this suggestion, including food spills ruining the gym floor and the need for more tables and chairs. It seemed that we were onto something, but there were still problems to iron out. The staff agreed to talk to their colleagues about the ramifications of this proposal.

The dynamics of solving the problem had completely changed. Now we were working together to make a solution work, rather than being divided about whether to tackle the subject. People really wanted to figure this thing out.

There were many conversations among the staff over the next few days. Teachers agreed to take turns supervising the overflow group of students in the gym, and sought Jamie's opinion. They explained the problem to her and described how everyone had joined to make it possible.

Jamie was understandably concerned about how to keep the floor clean, especially with youngsters scheduled for physical education right after lunch. She also pointed out that it would take a long time to move tables and chairs in and out of the gym. In addition, there was the problem of where to store the cafeteria tables and chairs when they were not in use. What seemed to be a big obstacle to others was one that I, as the principal, could solve. I offered to find folding tables with attached benches, as well as the funds to purchase them.

Jamie agreed to be part of the proposed solution. It meant additional work for her, because now she'd have to set up and take down tables and clean the gym floor in addition to her work in the cafeterias. Yet she was willing to help the staff achieve their goal of only two lunch periods. The staff now had the immense satisfaction of solving together what had been a very troublesome problem.

I had been willing to address the issues at a faculty meeting if the 1st-grade teachers were willing to state their problem to their colleagues. I believed that when they were ready to own it and state their case, they would be more likely to invest themselves in enlisting help to find a solution that would address everyone's concerns. The problem also would seem more compelling to colleagues if they heard it directly from the 1st-grade teachers. I wasn't going to be the person who would choose a schedule and force people to live with it. Even if I simply had been the one to present the issue to the faculty, it may very well have been seen as "Susan's problem with the lunch schedule." The staff was much more invested in solving a problem that affected their 1st-grade colleagues than they might have been in rectifying a scheduling problem presented by the principal.

There also were contractual issues involved. I would not have imposed lunch duty on people who were entitled to free time. Because the idea came from the group and the solution seemed the only way to remedy the problem, it was agreeable to the faculty. The teachers, invested in the outcome of this decision, were creative and cooperative about finding a solution and making it work.

As valuable as it is to find a solution to a presenting problem, it is just as important to recognize the importance of problem-solving and decision-making processes. It is often the leader's role to facilitate joint problem solving; it is equally important that the leader highlight what actually happened. In this way, the members of the school community can look back on their behaviors and see the ways in which their collaborations achieved the goal. They also can reflect on what parts of their interactions helped or hindered reaching the goal. Even if we ultimately had concluded that nothing would satisfy everyone's needs, at least we would have worked together to try to solve the problem. People may have become more empathic to the dilemma faced by the 1st-grade teachers, and perhaps the upper-grade teachers would have been more open to taking turns with the first lunch period or to finding some other compromise.

Our community was learning to take care of itself. Through the course of this meeting, my role as a leader was less obvious, because I provided modeling, momentum, hopefulness, and concern for relationships rather than direction or dismissal of the problem. Sometimes it's most effective for leaders to let the group's process unfold in its own way.

Promoting Teacher Leadership

I encouraged teachers to note what evoked their passion. What were they drawn to or whom? How did they express themselves when they were not self-censoring? What were their core values? As a leader, I noticed the talents and interests of individuals and acknowledged them. I tried to facilitate further exploration or use of these gifts. It was very exciting to watch staff members use their individual talents and interests to the benefit of the school community. As a principal, I sometimes offered resources, as well as the opportunity for the staff to implement their ideas.

When I first became a principal, my youth and some of the staff's intentionally hurtful behaviors toward me made it difficult for me to foster a culture of support. As time passed and my staying power became evident, teachers were more willing to work with me to address schoolwide issues. Once we pooled our resources, we achieved so much that they reluctantly began to concede that perhaps I could facilitate their growth through recognition of their skills and support of their initiatives.

In my second and third principalships, many staff members were much more receptive to my efforts to foster a collaborate culture, and we were able to do so much sooner. My role as a leader was often less visible, because I worked behind the scenes to promote the talents and endeavors of staff members. Sometimes my endorsement of their ideas was all that was required, and they virtually did the rest by themselves.

For example, an art teacher had the idea to feature students' creations throughout the town during the school year, as well as at special events. She and the other art teachers also came up with the idea of an art retrospective. Students wrote reflections on their art over their 5 years in school to accompany an exhibit of examples of their growth. The art teacher even triple-matted students' creations before displaying them, conveying her respect for their artwork. Families, teachers, and fellow students were enthralled.

Another teacher was remarkably adept at involving students in drama and musical productions that gave the youngsters opportunities to shine in ways that had not been revealed previously. Because the productions were of very high caliber, students were deservedly proud of their stage roles, as well as their involvement in such a valued school production.

In one school, two teachers were remarkably gifted in their ability to promote common goals by bringing the community together. For example, they organized a Turkey Trot, gathering the whole school population in the auditorium to lead everyone in song and warm-ups before they went outdoors to walk, jog, or run. They recruited parents to keep children safe by directing traffic in the neighborhood and supplying orange slices and water. One of the teachers even symbolized the community spirit they had fostered by appearing as a huge, brightly colored turkey. By appearing in costume, he stepped out of his own identity to serve as a unifying image.

Many other teachers made contributions to school communities in ways that were more subtle and less visible to everyone else. Their enthusiasm and responsiveness, their participation in the initiatives of their colleagues, and the way they inspired students in their classrooms were known and valued by the school community.

Mentoring new faculty is a very valuable contribution. Mentors spent countless hours familiarizing new colleagues with school culture and the expectations of the community. Teachers who weren't mentors often played crucial roles for new staff. One teacher organized a welcoming breakfast and provided the food, decorations, and party favors herself.

Teacher leadership that supports and nurtures is a large part of what builds such a strong sense of community. Identifying and acknowledging the specific talents of adults in the school helped them to share their gifts; this promoted their growth, as well as that of others.

You often can tell when the staff feel the support of their principal and peers by their motivation and the warm feeling that they exude throughout the school. Being recognized for their unique contributions and talents brings a deeper sense of acceptance and results in each person bringing more of themselves into their roles in the school. When staff experience being seen, known, and understood, the whole school can flourish.

CHAPTER FIVE

Advisers, Mentors, and Allies

When I was in kindergarten, my teacher thought I was a leader. I clearly remember a statement she made when we were preparing for our graduation ceremony. She appointed me to be the leader of the girls and Warren to be the leader of the boys. Then she said, "Girls, follow Susan. Warren, you follow Susan, too." My teacher confided that she was counting on me to lead the graduation procession and I just couldn't be absent. "People are counting on you." I took this comment very seriously and held onto that message long after I left kindergarten.

Being identified as the leader, aspiring to be one, or stepping into a leadership position is quite challenging. Identifying, finding, and accepting the support we need may have a big impact on our success. Support for a leader may come from a colleague, a parent, someone from the community, or a friend. Sometimes it even comes from a child. Support may be for the leader's feelings or may be about a current situation. Support may take the form of hand-holding, help in strategizing, modeling, or mentoring. Wherever we find it and whatever form it takes, it is crucial that we surround ourselves with enough of the kind of support we need to do our jobs well and to be who we are, which means knowing—or learning—what that is.

When I doubt myself, I like to look in a file I keep in my desk that contains letters of support. Reading the letters helps me remember that there are folks who appreciate me and value what I do. After a particularly trying episode at school one year, receiving the following letter from a parent (with a bag of jelly beans) made all the difference:

> It's your vision that attracts the excellent teachers and staff. . . . Your standards are high, you demand a great deal, and you want the best for your students, families, and teachers. . . . Like me, you are willing to take risks and therefore draw controversy. However, you handle controversy much better than I do. In fact . . . when I want to back away or ignore conflict, you encourage—and sometimes make—me deal with it. I treasure your ability to inspire me to rise to the occasion. . . . Because you can inspire and teach someone as stubborn as I am, I'm confident about your ability to lead the rest of the school.

One of the most crucial comments of support I've received was from the person who hired and then supervised me in my first principalship, the superintendent. During the many difficulties I faced when I began, his faith was a big part of what sustained me. When I went into his office to tell him that the faculty had filed a second grievance against me, my composure shattered, and I began to cry. "I don't know how this can be happening," I told him. "I'm trying so hard."

He reassured me by saying, "Sometimes getting a grievance is not because you are doing things wrong, but because you are doing things right!" To this day, I cannot imagine a more encouraging response. Knowing the superintendent could see beyond the turmoil of the moment and support my courage enabled me to use my energy to be a better leader.

Talking with close friends was another important support. How many hours I spent in a dear friend's kitchen, regaling her with my latest travails. I cried, and sometimes we laughed, as I told her what it was like trying to be a principal. Her consistent faith in me, as well as her outrage at what she was hearing about my new colleagues, helped sustain me through that gut-wrenching time.

It was at a workshop for administrators that I first heard about NECEL, the NorthEast Coalition of Education Leaders, which has contributed enormously to my evolution as a leader. During my first few agonizing years as a principal, I met women administrators who helped me understand—and withstand—my daily experiences. Many of us were grappling with how to get more women and other minorities into administrative jobs and then how to enable them to succeed in those jobs. NECEL members offered just what I needed at the time: support, advice, and new models of leadership.

One NECEL member was even a model for me about being a principal and starting a family. I literally ran to talk with her at a NECEL conference when I heard she had had a child, actually twins, and continued in her position.

Not only did NECEL contribute to my evolution as a leader, NECEL also had its own evolution, as NECEL members tried to communicate how we do the job differently. From this came NECEL's articulation of the five attributes of leadership: caring, collaboration, courage, intuition, and vision. Though I couldn't have articulated these attributes at the time, they reflected the traits in myself I called upon to be a leader. Had I known when I began my principalship that others, too, recognized these attributes as being at the core of leadership, I would have been more confident about openly using them in my new role. A relationship I had with a teacher during my first two years as a principal illustrates the power of these attributes.

Dolores disagreed with just about everything I did as the principal of the school. Her judgments often seemed harsh and undeserved. She was a very witty, charismatic person, and the combination of these qualities and her judgments often left me feeling defenseless and publicly shamed. For many months, I had a recurring dream that Dolores changed her opinion of me. Each time I awoke, I was confronted with the futility of my wish. I still find it hard to admit how much I hoped it would happen.

When Dolores casually mentioned her wish to leave teaching and begin a career in business, I offered to advise her on ways to move into the private sector. We talked about how she might present her credentials, and I told her the benefits of "information interviewing." I also told her I had no doubt she would be successful in her new career.

Weeks later, Dolores told me how much the information interviewing was helping her break into the field. That afternoon I got a note, spontaneously written on yellow classroom paper:

"You know so much. What a waste of two years."

I couldn't believe my eyes. I probably blinked to make sure I wasn't asleep. Dolores had acknowledged my strengths! Had

I withheld my knowledge and advice, she never would have expressed what I had wanted so badly to hear her say. Though I couldn't have articulated the NECEL attributes at the time, they reflected how I worked.

My vision of a school community was that all members would find their work satisfying and fulfilling and would receive colleagues' support toward this end, regardless of their personal feelings about the individuals. Intuitively I sensed that this could be a way to begin the kind of respectful relationship Dolores and I had not been able to have before. My caring took the form of offering advice and knowledge beyond my responsibility as a principal. It took courage to offer assistance to Dolores. It took even more courage not merely to advise her, but also to offer to collaborate with her in her next steps.

These attributes of leadership are often present in leaders who are nontraditional. Whether it is men or women who are new administrators, people of color, or administrators who seek alternative ways to lead, NECEL's five attributes of leadership may be both affirming and instructive.

DEMONSTRATING CARING

Although people had recognized these attributes of leadership in me in other ways throughout my life, my path to leadership in public elementary schools has been a little unusual. School administration had never been my dream.

In my late teens, I had strongly resisted my mother's urging to become a teacher. I kept saying that I didn't want to work only with women and children, resisting a career that was typically prescribed for my gender. I felt like I should "do something more."

I had been led to believe, by my parents and teachers, that I was intelligent and talented and that I was capable of excelling in a prestigious field. Because society didn't hold the teaching profession in high esteem, I closed myself off from the idea of teaching, intuiting that no matter how well I performed, I would not be sufficiently recognized for my achievement.

At my father's suggestion, I majored in business administration in college and discovered that I was one of only two female students in the department. When I was about to graduate, I heard that women were not being offered management-training positions but instead had to take secretarial jobs and work their way up. I was so outraged by that idea that I decided to get a master's degree in higher education administration, mistakenly believing that gender discrimination would not be a factor at the college level.

Yet when I applied to graduate school, I did so in elementary education. How did that happen when I was so adamant about not wanting to be a teacher? Perhaps in a time of uncertainty, I went back to what seemed safe and familiar: my mother's suggestion to become a teacher.

In my second year of teaching 1st grade, I offered to teach our newly appointed principal about the educational needs of young children and to give him feedback on his entry into our school community. He welcomed my offer and I unknowingly took another step toward becoming a principal myself. His acknowledgment that I knew more than he about early childhood education, as well as the interpersonal dynamics of our school, affirmed my self-confidence and empowered me to begin to think of myself as an educational leader.

During the next few years, that principal and the superintendent told me that I would be an excellent principal. I scoffed at the idea. When they insisted, I told them that I loved teaching 1st grade and that I thought administration was a horrible job. It was too bad that they had to do it, I said, but I was perfectly content where I was. They persisted, and at one point the superintendent said something that resonated within me: "If you value community as much as you seem to, you could influence a larger community as a principal than you could as a teacher of one class."

The idea that I could influence an entire school community was very enticing. At one point the superintendent predicted that I would move on within a year or two and said that was the reason that he canceled my presentation to the school committee of my proposal for a teacher center.

In fact, one year later I was appointed to a principalship in a neighboring state. I was amazed that the superintendent had known me better than I knew myself. How could he have foreseen my future when I was so unaware of my growing interest in school administration? The effect that principal and superintendent had on my career development and aspirations was significant. They clearly saw something in me that I hadn't seen in myself.

SEEKING OR ACCEPTING SUPPORT

Sometimes there is someone who has a vision of us that surpasses our current aspirations. Gail Sheehy calls this heightened vision "the Dream." People may support us in this journey to realize our Dream without our initial awareness that they are doing it.

During my first principalship, I was invited to join the Education Subcommittee of the Governor's Advisory Commission on Women. I didn't know what prompted the invitation, but I was intrigued and delighted. I needed a change of pace and an opportunity to think about education in a more global way. The women I met at the first meeting were dynamic and articulate. They were doing all kinds of interesting things throughout the state, in many roles and institutions.

Before I knew it, I was offered support for an endeavor I had only briefly mentioned. A liaison from the state Department of Education offered to provide technical assistance and funding for our Career Exploration Program. I jumped at the offer.

It was only afterward, when I was asked to write a booklet describing this endeavor as a model for the state, that I found out that I had been recommended specifically for support. The chair of the Education Subcommittee of the Governor's Advisory Commission on Women had chosen to sponsor me. When I think about the camaraderie and support I received from the members of the Education Subcommittee, I still feel a deep sense of protection because, despite what was happening at my school, I had these strong and accomplished women on my side.

The image of a mentor who comes to the rescue of a confused novice represents, I believe, a longing that some of us have felt. While novices want to be effective, they may not always know how. Mentors can help them learn to do so with confidence.

My research on mentoring for my doctoral dissertation entailed interviewing women administrators and their mentors. I heard about mentoring relationships that lasted for many years, through the ups and downs of their careers.

Some of us are fortunate enough to have a mentor, someone who consistently believes in our capability and commits to working with us to further our professional growth. A mentor is someone who combines the skills and caring of a professional colleague, supporter, and ally with knowledge about ways our talents may be utilized professionally. A mentor works with us in the hard times, because a mentor is respectful of our positive intention and capacity to contribute. A mentor is mindful, however, that people are complex and, therefore, leadership involves complex interactions. So a mentor is patient about the time it takes to sort out complicated issues.

Having a mentor is especially helpful in situations in which a person needs coaching and support from someone who knows the terrain but isn't the evaluator. Hearing that another person has had similar experiences or understands the dynamics is immensely reassuring, especially when we are doubting our capability. Learning how others have handled similar situations can be very helpful so that we don't have to reinvent the wheel while we are in the middle of the ride.

I have not had that experience. Perhaps it did not seem to others that I would want a mentor. My poise and determination may have concealed from prospective mentors my longing for a consistently supportive collegial relationship in which my growth was the focus. Sometimes there are a variety of people who encourage or provide assistance in specific ways at various points in our career.

In my first principalship, a member of the school committee offered me a special kind of support. Estelle was a former school principal, and she could see what I was trying to achieve, perhaps more clearly than I, because I was so heavily entangled in the daily struggles. Estelle would acknowledge the harassment, knowingly nod with regret about the situation, and then add that she was confident that my administration would prove to be just what the school needed. Estelle didn't inquire about my feelings. She didn't give me advice or teach me specific skills or strategies. Rather, Estelle steadfastly affirmed that, of course, I and my leadership would prevail.

Estelle was an unusual person with a noteworthy style. When she spoke, she enunciated each word and commanded attention. In so doing, for some she projected sophistication and intellectual authority. For others, there was an uncertainty about her credibility. Although Estelle rose above it, I believe she sensed their uninformed disdain. I believe Estelle empathized with my isolation and wanted to support me even though—and perhaps because—I, too, was different. I could feel Estelle's fondness for me and received tangible evidence of it when she knitted two sweaters for my newborn.

I missed an opportunity to learn from Estelle by not opening up more. With so many people speaking about what I couldn't do, I think it may have felt too risky to reveal my pain and confusion to one of the few people who had confidence in me. I didn't want to chance losing Estelle's vision of me.

In thinking about the people in my life who have assisted me for shorter periods of time, I have concluded that, for some of them, part of their interest in working with me came from their wish to support my ideas about leadership and education. For others, it was because I used what they said to me and worked very hard to achieve my goals.

A person who made this clear to me was Kirt, a director of career development, who helped me with my resume when I was applying for my first principalship. I remember Kirt being very blunt with me. "This is a great resume if you want to get another job teaching first grade." I had not expected this feedback and felt deflated, but then Kirt told me what I needed to do to strengthen my resume and help get me the principalship I sought.

I went home and worked on my resume for a couple of days and called him back. "I've redone my resume based on your suggestions. Would you be willing to look at it and tell me what you think?" We met, and Kirt helped me put the finishing touches on the document. Then he talked with me about interviewing.

I had thought that interviewing would be a strength of mine, but again Kirt gave me some unexpected feedback. "You don't look like a principal, at least not the kind most people are used to seeing. You smile too much and you are very soft-spoken. People are going to think that you will be too soft." I wanted to point out that Kirt was describing the stereotypes of a principal, but I realized that he was probably right about the first impression I would make on screening committees.

"Just because I smile doesn't mean I can't be tough when I have to," I responded, probably trying to convince myself as much as him.

"You know," Kirt said, "you lowered your voice a whole octave when you said that. I believed you. If you say it just that way in your interviews, I think they'll believe you too." I took his advice and, during interviews, even made a point of speaking about my demeanor before being asked. By initiating communication about my manner, I probably helped allay interviewers' doubts about my ability to be a disciplinarian when it was necessary. Of course, later I would show them that I had very different ideas about discipline, but at least my initial presentation wouldn't keep them from envisioning me as a principal.

I met with Kirt several more times, and he spent a fair amount of time with me at each meeting. Finally, I couldn't contain my curiosity. "I'm wondering why you spend so much time with me," I said. "You don't know me from a hole in the wall."

"I know enough about you to want to help you, and that is because you take my advice and work hard to use my suggestions." He continued, "Other people come in, 'yeah yeah' me, and then when they come back they complain about the same things. Have they done anything I said? No. They just want someone to listen to them whine. I feel like the time I give you is well spent."

As Kirt articulated why he was advising me, I realized that other people probably also had valued my responsiveness to their coaching and my willingness to work hard to improve myself. Their offers of help hadn't just come out of the blue. Learning this enabled me to seek and accept assistance with a greater understanding of what inspires mentors to make such a strong commitment.

With Kirt, as with so many people and situations in my life, I worked very hard. I always tried to be planful and diligent, yet I was able to remain open to unexpected opportunities. Having a mind-set of hope made it possible for me to respond to serendipitous situations, and my sense of possibility was further reinforced.

At difficult times, I have hoped for encouragement or affirmation for taking considered risks from advisers, allies, and friends. When I received the unexpected fallout from my letter about swimming and self-acceptance, I hoped that trusted colleagues would support my decision. Instead, I found that colleagues who cared a great deal about my well-being were more concerned about the potential negative consequences of my act than about what was to be gained. Instead of naming their fear of my being hurt, their fear about it did the talking. The message I received was "There are dangers inherent in this endeavor, so don't do it." They made a judgment about my action, based on the reaction I'd received instead of the value of what I did.

I had more courage than they did at that time. I would have appreciated hearing someone say, "This an important letter. If you are prepared to take the fallout (and there will be fallout), stand by your decision. Do it and I'm behind you." Had I a mentor, perhaps I would have received that response; sometimes mentors can offer what close colleagues cannot.

As important as mentors and supporters are to us, we ourselves often know more than we may realize, but we must get quiet and listen. When I mentor, I encourage people to listen to their inner voices. We discuss the possible ramifications of any endeavor, and sometimes I suggest another approach that would help them achieve their objectives without putting themselves in jeopardy. I work to help them think about whether the risks they are contemplating are worth taking. I urge them to explore what "feels right," and I advise them to use their courage carefully but certainly to take the risks that they believe they must.

THE SERENDIPITY OF MUTUAL MENTORING

In my doctoral research, one respondent adamantly resisted identifying mentors in her career, feeling that the term connoted positional power that was not reflective of any relationships she had. She acknowledged the importance of some key people in her career yet insisted the relationships were not based on a higher-up/lower-down structure, in which one was the mentor and the other was the grateful recipient. Instead, she described collegial and equal relationships.

Many people think this mutuality cannot occur when mentors are also evaluators, because of the confusion that this added dimension will have on the relationship. Although I agree, I have mentored a number of staff members at schools where I was principal, because some teachers specifically sought me out. With them, I have developed deeper relationships because of their interest in working more closely with me on their professional development, remaining cognizant of the times when my supervisory role may have had to take precedence.

One person with whom I shared a more mutual mentoring relationship was an unsuccessful inside candidate for the principalship I obtained in her school. Josie was very intelligent, sensitive, and talented, and she had been a part of the system for a long time. The superintendent told her he didn't think she was quite ready to be the principal and that she should learn from me once I arrived. Who learned the most is debatable.

Josie knew the staff, she knew the children, she knew the system, and she knew the town. As an added bonus, she knew a lot more about technology than I did. In many ways, Josie seemed to me to be the perfect candidate for the principalship, although I wouldn't have had the chance to meet her had the superintendent seen it that way.

Flowers sent by Josie greeted me when I first arrived on the job. She was up front about her aspirations to be a principal and candid about her experience of applying for the position I now occupied. She wanted to learn, and I was happy to teach her anything I could. As it became clear how much Josie was orienting me and advising me about situations at the school, I was even more delighted to reciprocate.

There are probably strategies I helped her learn, though I think she would have been able to figure them out herself. Perhaps the way I most helped Josie grow was by processing with her the events at school and the staff's reactions to my leadership. Although Josie might have done things differently herself, she got to observe what happened when I did something my way. She saw how her colleagues responded to initiatives that she and I thought made sense, as well as how I processed it all. These were the things that Josie and I could discuss as we reviewed the day's events. We speculated about how the faculty would react to a different way of leading; Josie was able to imagine reactions and then see what actually happened.

Because many of the staff were Josie's longtime friends, I imagine that she heard a much more candid version of people's reactions than I ever did. (Josie was actually in an even better position to evaluate what was happening than I was.) My reactions may have been helpful to Josie because I was new to a system she had been a part of for a long time. Sometimes we encountered difficulties when some of the staff disagreed with initiatives or reacted to a way of leading that was new at this school. Sometimes we took detours along the way or even changed our course as we obtained new information, but Josie saw that we continued to move forward.

I respected Josie's professionalism immensely. She was always interested in what was best for the children, she respected people's confidences, and her only agendas at school were to learn and to be of service to the school community. I wanted to do anything I could to assist her in reaching her professional goals.

I told her about NECEL and encouraged her to join. We discussed the relative merits for her career of attending various workshops or conferences. I offered Josie my experience as a principal and Josie was a translator, ambassador, and special adviser to me.

When it was time for our school to be evaluated for accreditation by a visiting team, I appointed Josie as the chair of the steering committee. I knew she had the organizational, communication, and analytical skills the job required, and I thought it would be a great opportunity for her to "show her stuff" in this leadership role. Of course, it did not escape me that she would do a tremendous job.

She could see that I was the kind of leader who didn't feel the need to have everything figured out in advance. I actually had volunteered for our school to become accredited, although it was not typical for elementary schools. My faith in the benefits of a self-evaluation process was confirmed, although I couldn't have predicted how.

Our staff was insightful in evaluating our school, the staff, the community, and our programs. Josie got staff members on board who might not have participated as fully had she not been there to request their involvement. Some of the teachers may have been nervous about participating in a school accreditation, but Josie knew how to make them comfortable. By the time the visiting team arrived, Josie had put them at ease.

We got rave reviews and commendations from the visiting team. Soon after, Josie obtained her first principalship in another school district. I had been very pleased to speak with that superintendent about Josie when she was one of the finalists, and I was so enthusiastic about her that the superintendent commented on the intensity of my high regard.

Josie became a different kind of principal. She once made a deal with the students of her school that if they read a certain number of books, she would dress up in the costume of their choice and spend a day on the roof of the school. Josie helped motivate the students to read more books, and she kept her promise: She dressed as an astronaut, and up she went.

When a critical letter about her actions was printed in the town paper, the outcry from the community was deafening. There were so many letters of support for Josie during the following weeks that she was close to canonization. I was delighted. She was clearly a principal with a unique way of leading, and it was gratifying to see that her constituencies valued her for it.

My role as a mentor had been to validate her talents and encourage her to take the risks to be a principal in her own way. Seeing her do this gave me the satisfaction many mentors experience as they watch talented women and men assume leadership.

PASSING THE TORCH
AND SHARING ITS LIGHT

When I mentor, I sometimes teach how to do things, like preparing a budget or writing a proposal. Other times, I share my experiences before and after becoming a principal, to give a picture of what various aspects of the job are actually like. I sometimes mentor administrative aspirants in their practica and internships; through working together on projects, the interns and I are able to combine theoretical and practical information in ways that can be useful to different constituencies in a school community. In each context of mentoring, we often spend most of our time debriefing events or discussing dilemmas, with an eye toward developing and refining strategies. Seeing how the principal acts in a situation and then reviewing with the principal how it went provides insight into both people's thoughts about leadership.

In the process of mentoring, mentors benefit from hearing other perspectives, as well as from the questions they are asked. Mentors often have to clarify and expand their own understanding in order to respond to inquiries about their actions. Mentoring provides an opportunity for mentors to reflect on their own professional growth. It is often very satisfying for mentors to see themselves through the eyes of people at various stages of their careers. It feels good to help other people learn and move forward, and I sometimes receive from them the same things I offer: a sense of belonging, opportunities for growth, and support for risk taking.

Good mentors are in high demand. There are many more people who seek such a relationship than could possibly be accommodated. In addition, it may be more difficult to find, in one person, all the attributes and knowledge we desire in a mentor. Although it would be a joy to have the concentrated attention and support of a mentor who offers it all, we can successfully piece together what we need from different people. I have. It's like grazing throughout the day, even though sometimes it would be luscious to have a feast at one table.

A way that some colleagues and I have brought such richness into our lives is to meet for a weekend once a year. These colleagues are women I know from NECEL. One of them astutely observed that we always were so busy organizing conferences and attending to all the details that we never got a chance to finish our own conversations. After our first weekend, it was clear that we wanted to ensure that this would be an annual event. In this group of women, whose ages, lifestyles, and careers are very different, we support, gently tease, and encourage one another.

Whether in a group or individually, leaders can cultivate these relationships. We can do this by carefully choosing people in whom to confide and share experiences, by listening and following up on what they have said, and by letting them know their impact on us.

Even though some mentoring relationships can go on for a long time, we must realize that our efforts to promote the growth and professional development of people we mentor may result in their departure. Teachers I have mentored have moved on to become principals, to raise children, and to pursue other careers. I believe that it is my responsibility as an educator to encourage them to take the next steps they envision. In fact, there have been times when I have suggested endeavors that capitalized on or expanded someone's talents, knowing that person might leave teaching as a result. Although it may be a great loss when they leave, I also feel pleasure and delight for them.

I feel strongly about my responsibility to help aspiring administrators, especially women joining the profession. Just as others have given to me, I enjoy being able to continue the cycle of support and coaching. It feels very satisfying to pass the torch.

Writing this book felt like a new way for me to mentor, although it is primarily with people I will not meet. When I was just starting out, I would have loved it if people had shared with me what they had learned in their years as principals. I still find it enlightening to hear how others deal with situations similar to those in which I found myself. The knowledge of how useful it can be to share stories has kindled and fanned my desire to share my craft wisdom through writing.

The writing and publishing of this book has been a journey in itself—a journey of exploration, of priorities, of decision making. For me, it brought a new level of thinking, learning, and expressing, and a new stage in my growth and evolution as a leader. One of the reasons I wanted to write this book is that I believe leaders have a responsibility to continue growing and to contribute to the profession. It was a risk, and I knew that the process of writing a book would require some of the very leadership abilities I was discussing.

I sent my book proposal to publishers and was excited when I was offered a contract. Believing in relational leadership as much as I do, I was naturally concerned about the possible impact of my writing on people I know or have known in the past. How might other people remember the events? How might they interpret what I wrote? Would they agree with my opinions or analysis? Might someone feel threatened by my writing the stories at all? Speaking from the best of my recollection and understanding was the best safeguard I could offer.

I hope that by writing this book, I inspire people to value and trust their talents and strengths, to envision their own leadership, to reflect on their practice, and to be emboldened to act authentically.

CHAPTER SIX

Reflecting on a Career

Committing to Pursue Professional Passion

A parent told her son that she could never be a principal because it's one of the hardest jobs she knew, to which he replied "But Mom, Dr. Villani always has a smile on her face everywhere!"

AM I IN THE RIGHT PLACE
DOING THE WORK I WANT TO BE DOING?

How do we know whether we are working in the right place, the place where we can make our best contribution, and the place where we are nourished, energized, and growing? Is place a specific school or district, or is it a role?

What are some of the factors principals consider when choosing where they want to be a principal? Through personal experience, what others have told me, and reading, I offer the following:

- What is the setting of the school?

    Is it urban, rural, or suburban? Keep in mind that urban systems are not only found in big cities, and that some districts have combinations of settings within their districts.

Is this setting a place in which you would enjoy living? Is there a nearby town or city you might prefer?

- What is the size of the school?

  If it's a large school, is it subdivided into houses, teams, or departments?

- What is the district size?

  Is the district centrally operated, or is there site-based management?

  Do principals and staff have a lot of autonomy or are they directed largely by systemwide initiatives?

- Is there an administrative team, possibly including assistant principals, deans of students, or department chairs?

  Some administrators prefer having at least one other administrator on site with whom to share responsibilities. At the elementary level, the size of the school may be the deciding factor on whether there is an assistant principal.

- What are the demographics of the school community and town?

- What is the socioeconomic status of the school population, and is it diverse socioeconomically?

- What is the racial/ethnic/religious makeup of the students and their families?

- What is the racial/ethnic/religious makeup of the school staff?

  Sometimes principals want to serve a community composed of people of their own ethnicity/race or religion. Many principals are eager to work with any or all races. Often school systems are eager to diversify their faculty and administration and are hoping to recruit principals who will contribute to this diversity. If a school or district recruits someone whose ethnic or racial identify is other than the majority of the population, the candidate needs to consider whether she or he will enjoy working and possibly living in this setting. For example, suburban school system efforts to recruit diverse staff have sometimes been unsuccessful because the city or town does not offer the quality of life the new principal desires and this, in addition to the professional work setting, may strongly affect his or her wish to remain in the position. Responses to these issues are highly individual, and there are many examples of the matches being very successful.

- How much fiscal support does the school receive?

  What is the per-pupil expenditure?

  Does the town/city demonstrate the ability to provide the resources requested by the school administrators?

  As an administrator, how important is this to you? Some principals thrive on working within their communities to build support for their school or finding other funding sources.

- What are identified community resources?

  Is there a lot of parent/family involvement in the schools?

  Is there a college or university in the town?

  Is there any industry or small business support of the schools?

- What issues have the townspeople/state/district identified as priorities for the schools?

- What talents and skills might you bring that would supplement what has already been achieved?

- Do you feel comfortable here, with the teachers, administrators, and central office administrators? (I didn't mention comfort with the students because it has always been my experience to enjoy the students. If that isn't a given, an important question would be "Do you want to serve these students?")

- Do you sense that you could feel trusting of this community?

- Do you think you would have some fun here?

The answers to these questions may help you decide where you would want your first principalship, or whether you might want a different setting for a second principalship. You might decide that you would like to work in a similar district, or that you would like to try something different.

Sometimes principals consider changing schools or systems because of a shift in philosophy as articulated by the superintendent or school board. If there comes a time when a principal's philosophy is not shared by the majority of the school community, then the principal has a decision to make: either move closer to what the community feels it needs or find a school community in which the match is more congruent. There is no shame in changing schools or districts to find a match that is more satisfying for your purposes and talents. Some of the most respected educational leaders have left their positions in times of rancor, strong emotion, or even chaos over disagreements about priorities, values, or goals. In fact, people have often been respected for taking a stand about their assumptions, beliefs, and values when they differ from what the current administration is espousing and for acting on their need to find a more congruent work environment.

Perhaps you are thinking of a principalship as a step toward becoming a district or central office administrator, such as the director of curriculum and instruction, director of human resources, assistant superintendent, or superintendent. What skills would you bring to these roles? What challenges would most interest you? Would you enjoy the responsibility of an entire school district, working with other administrators, staff, and community to articulate and realize a vision? Don't feel pushed to "advance" to the central office. Many principals find that a school is where they want to put their energies, and some have left central office positions to return to principalships.

Give yourself permission to consider the possibility of a variety of ways to share your craft wisdom. Principals learn so much during the course of their principalships that they are often very well prepared to share their knowledge and skills in other arenas of education. Some possibilities are

- Classroom teacher, PreK–12
- College or university instructor or full professor
- Executive director or staff member of an educational consortium
- State Department of Education staff member
- Consultant, independent or affiliated with an organization
- Student teacher supervisor
- Principal internship adviser

- Coach of teacher leaders, perhaps encouraging them toward a principalship
- Author of books or articles
- Speaker
- School committee member

Reflecting on our career and considering other roles in education is natural and necessary. Angel Nieto Romero (2000, p. iv) concludes his poem "To Be a Teacher" this way:

> To learn, to share, to teach
>
> and to learn again.
>
> To discover, to shape, to achieve
>
> And then to start all over again.

Source: Romero, Angel N. (2000). In Nieto, S., *Affirming Diversity* (p. iv). Addison Wesley Longman Publisher. Used with permission.

I believe these actions also apply to principals.

MY CHOICES AND YOURS

After this book was first published in 1999, Robb Clouse, my editor at the time, asked whether I might like to write more books for Corwin Press. I really wanted to say yes, and yet I knew that I could not find the energy and time to keep writing while I was also a principal, mother, and wife. It had taken intense concentration to write this book, and I didn't think I could summon that discipline and focus again in the near future.

I realized I was at a choice point. Like most important decisions, this one was multifaceted. The factors I considered were my family, my career, and my passion. I had chosen to become a principal when I was single. I don't think I realized the number of hours I would spend in my job, and that has greatly expanded during the tenure of my three principalships.

During my career, I had two children. While the tug I felt about not being with my children during the day was the most obvious when they were very young, it turned out that I was the most concerned about them as they got older. When they were in high school, they often had moved from thinking about school to another plane of consciousness by the time I got home and were less inclined to talk with me about what they were thinking and feeling. I was missing the conversations we used to have at a time that seemed so important for us to stay connected. Not being home when they returned from school was weighing heavily on my thoughts. I reasoned that if I was there in the afternoons they might be more inclined to share some of their experiences and feelings about school and friends with me before retreating to their rooms to listen to music, talk on the telephone, and do homework.

I also needed to think about my feelings as a principal. Our school had made great progress in the 11 years I was there. The students seemed to be thriving, academically and socially. We had advanced from being the elementary school in town with the lowest test scores to the one with the highest. I had hired a number of very talented staff and they had become strong members of the faculty. The school had nearly doubled in size, and despite my warnings that we would not be able to provide as much individualized service to a doubled population, in fact we did.

While I valued my career as a principal and was proud of the impact of our collective efforts, I wondered whether now might be the time to use my talents and energies elsewhere. I stuck my toe in the water and mentioned my thought of leaving the principalship to my husband. He had encouraged me to consider pursuing the college teaching and consulting that I had enjoyed to a very limited extent while I was a principal. Being a principal doesn't afford much time for other work. I had been an adjunct professor for years, teaching an outreach course or two a year on weekends. I had consulted a bit with a few other districts about mentoring new teachers and found it very rewarding. Working with experienced staff to support new teachers is a way to share craft wisdom. As I reflected on my choices, I realized I was feeling energized by the possibilities of change.

Of course, I found it difficult to think about not being a principal after doing so for 21 years. I had just written a book about being a principal, and I was considering leaving that role. Still, the thought of writing another book, teaching college courses, and consulting was very appealing. Perhaps writing the book prompted and enabled me to live the final chapter in that role and explore other ways to support students' and adults' growth.

As the title of a popular book on career development advises, "Do what you love and the money will follow" (Sinetar, 1989). Charlie Parker once said, "If it ain't in your heart, it ain't in your horn" (http://media.wiley.com/assets/45/45/0787958026_Palmer .pdf). I never presumed that if I changed my thinking about where I would make my best contribution in education suddenly other types of work would appear. Yet that is what happened. I entered a contract with Corwin to write a book about mentoring programs for new teachers and I reestablished my connection with the university at which I had been an adjunct professor. To my surprise and utter delight, they created a half-time position for me to teach master's degree candidates courses on equity and action research. A few months later, I was invited to interview at Learning Innovations at WestEd, and I accepted a part-time position as senior program/research associate with them. I couldn't believe my good fortune. "It's not just good luck" people would say to me. "All that you have done these past 28 years has prepared you well and may have led you to take this next path."

A parent wrote the following about change and moving forward when I announced my resignation from my third and last principalship:

> For us it will be strongly felt in the fall when you are not there to begin with us again. However, change is inevitable and exists in the ongoing partnership with life—creation and re-creation. It is difficult to conceive that which lies beyond the energy of the sun, so as it may be difficult for us to let go of that with which we are comfortable. We can again look to you and be reminded to go forward with life and its changes, success being guaranteed when one's heart is in the right place.

For me, working in education has been a spiral that continues to circle back and move forward. I learned a great deal during my years as a principal and a classroom teacher and as a result have earned credibility with educators I now meet in my work. While writing *Mentoring Programs for New Teachers: Models of Induction and Support,* I did the majority of my work at Learning Innovations in school districts and states, facilitating the development of mentoring programs for new teachers and offering professional development to mentors, new teachers, and literacy and math coaches. A colleague at Learning Innovations and I have coauthored a book and facilitator training guide titled *Mentoring New Teachers Through Collaborative Coaching: Linking Teacher and Student Learning*

My interest in supporting new principals resulted in my writing *Mentoring and Induction Programs That Support New Principals,* a topic related to my doctoral dissertation, and am now doing more work to support new principals. I know what it is like to be a principal and a classroom teacher. I recall quite vividly the challenges they face, and the issues they may encounter along the way. I love to mentor new principals and new teachers. I am thrilled when I can help others learn to coach principals or help teachers to reflect on their practice and improve it. It is such an honor to support them.

I had included the following message for aspiring and new principals at the end of the first edition of this book when it was published in 1999. I find that Marianne Williamson's (1992, p. 165) words are equally applicable to principals evaluating their careers or contemplating a career shift.

> Our deepest fear is not that we are inadequate. Our deepest fear is that we are powerful beyond measure. It is our light, not our darkness, that most frightens us. We ask ourselves, who am I to be brilliant, gorgeous, talented, and fabulous? Actually, who are you not to be? Your playing small doesn't serve the world. There's nothing enlightened about shrinking so that other people won't feel insecure around you. . . . And as we let our own light shine, we unconsciously give other people permission to do the same. As we are liberated from our own fear, our presence automatically liberates others.

My wish for you is that you choose work that makes your heart sing and continue to do it as long as it does. If you ever ask yourself whether you want to continue with your principalship, I hope you will listen. If you need to make a change, I hope you do it. You may decide to stay, and if you do I think you will find that you bring a different outlook after having recommitted to your work. For the sake of our schools, I hope that many of you will say, "Yes, I am sure I am the principal, and this is what I want to do."

People Whose
Work Is Featured
in the Study Guides

The following educational researchers and writers are cited in connection with key ideas in the book:

Roland Barth is the founding director of the Principals' Center at Harvard University and has written numerous articles and books, including *Lessons Learned: Shaping Relationships and the Culture of the Workplace* and *Improving Schools From Within*.

Marian Wright Edelman is the president of the Children's Defense Fund. Among her articles and books are *The Measure of Our Success* and *Guide My Feet*.

Richard Elmore is Gregory R. Anrig Professor of Educational Leadership at Harvard University and director of the Consortium for Policy Research in Education. He has written *Building a New Structure for School Leadership* and *Bridging the Gap Between Standards and Achievement*, as well as many other books and articles.

Jeffrey Glanz is the dean of Graduate Programs and chair of the Department of Education at Wagner College, where he coordinates the educational leadership program that leads to New York State certifications as a principal or assistant principal. He has written widely, including *What Every Principal Should Know About Leadership: The 7 Book Collection*.

Daniel Goleman is CEO of Emotional Intelligence Services. Among his several books is *Emotional Intelligence*. He has covered behavioral and brain sciences for the *New York Times*.

Ronald Heifitz is codirector of the Center for Public Leadership at the John F. Kennedy School of Government at Harvard University.

Among his articles and books are *Leadership on the Line: Staying Alive Through the Dangers of Leading* and *Leadership Without Easy Answers.*

Linda Lambert is founder of the Center for Educational Leadership at California State University, Hayward, where she is professor emeritus. Examples of her many articles and books are *Leadership Capacity for Lasting School Improvement* and *Building Leadership Capacity in Schools.*

Peggy McIntosh is associate director for the Wellesley College Research on Woman and founder and codirector of the National S.E.E.D. (Seeking Educational Equity and Diversity) Project on Inclusive Curriculum. Peggy McIntosh's work, "Feeling Like a Fraud," continues to be quoted and discussed decades after she first introduced her thinking.

Lorraine Monroe became principal of Harlem's Frederick Douglass School, which was well known for violence, poor attendance, and a low level of academic achievement. Five years later, student test scores ranked it among New York City's best high schools.

Nel Noddings is Jacks Professor Emerita of Child Education at Stanford University. She has written seminal works on the ethics of care, including *Challenge to Care in Schools* and *Educating Moral People.*

Thomas Sergiovanni is Lillian Radford Professor of Education at Trinity University. Among his works on this topic are *The Principalship: A Reflective Practice Perspective* and *Rethinking Leadership.*

Margaret (Meg) Wheatley is president of the Berkana Institute, a principal in Kellner-Rogers Wheatley, Inc., and a former professor of management at Brigham Young University. She is the author of *Leadership in the New Science.*

Andrew Young was a representative from Georgia to the U.S. Congress. He was the executive director of the Southern Christian Leadership Conference and U.S. ambassador to the United Nations.

Quotations from their work provide additional perspectives and educational knowledge connected with my stories about being a principal.

The study guides are presented in two parts:

1. Concepts about leadership that pertain to all chapters

2. Specific quotes and questions for each chapter

While I have written this book in the first person, describing my experiences, I have written the questions in the study guides to promote discussion about "the principal." The questions are framed to apply to the stories as case studies. The value to readers of self-reflection or discussion is in thinking about the principalship.

Study Guide
for All Chapters

The following quotes and questions may provoke thought as you read and reflect on each chapter.

Nel Noddings wrote, "The traditional organization of schooling is intellectually and morally inadequate for contemporary society" (p. 173). Her challenge is "We should educate all our children not only for competence but also for caring. Our aim should be to encourage the growth of competent, caring, loving, and lovable people" (p. xiv).

1. What are some examples of the principal's ethic of caring?

2. How might being familiar with Noddings's concept that leadership has an ethic of caring have informed the principal's thinking and behavior?

3. Noddings believes that we should educate all children not only for competence, but also for caring. Why would that matter?

4. In what ways might Noddings's comments on the ethic of caring inform your practice or be worth sharing with colleagues?

Jeffrey Glanz (p. 18) wrote that ethical leaders might ask themselves the following questions:

- What are the beliefs and values that I would fight for?
- How might I best communicate beliefs and values to my faculty and staff?

- How do I reconcile different beliefs and values with my own?
- How do I react in a crisis?
- Do I involve others in the decision-making process?
- Do I consider the perspective of the other?
- Am I caring and sensitive to others' feelings?
- Do I demonstrate by deed that I care?
- How do I know I'm doing a good job as a leader?

1. In what ways do you think these questions square with the principal's intentions/actions with staff, families, and students?

2. How does the concept of ethical leadership apply to your thinking and practice?

3. In what ways might Glanz's questions inform your practice or be worth sharing with colleagues?

Study Guides for Individual Chapters

STUDY GUIDE FOR CHAPTER 1: ARE YOU SURE YOU'RE THE PRINCIPAL?

Richard Elmore wrote, "Leadership tends to be romanticized in American culture, especially in the culture of schooling, both because we subscribe heavily to trait theory of success—people succeed because of their personal characteristics, more than because of effort, skill, and knowledge—and because we like our heroes to have qualities that we think we don't have. The problem with this romanticized theory of leadership is that the supply of character traits we associate with 'good' leaders is, by definition, limited, or we wouldn't envy and admire them so much in other people. Also, character traits are much less amenable to influence by education, training, and practice than are knowledge and skill. De-romanticizing leadership would have a very positive effect on the quality of schools" (pp. 13–14).

1. In what ways did the principal begin/grow/change with regard to this concept of heroes?

2. How might Elmore's idea have helped the principal understand what was happening to her and how she might respond or be proactive?

3. There are defining moments in any principalship and one of them is the first major decision made in a public forum.

Describe a leader's defining moment that you have witnessed or how you experienced your first major decision as a leader.

4. In what ways might Elmore's concept of romanticizing leaders inform your practice or be worth sharing with colleagues?

Lorraine Monroe (1999, p. 230) wrote, "Leaders are lonely, because they must think and dream about their work—all day, every day, day after day. Then they must make what they think and dream about understandable to people who haven't thought and dreamed as deeply, or as far into the future, as they have. They must believe in the dream and in the need to pursue it, and they must do the hard work of never doubting its importance. Doubts will arise—but the leader's job is to master those doubts and to press on."

1. How do you think the principal would have felt about Lorraine Monroe's view of the work of the principal?

2. Do you agree with Monroe that it is the principal's job to make what he or she thinks and dreams understandable to people who haven't thought and dreamed as deeply? Why or why not?

3. How does Lorraine Monroe's reflection that leaders are lonely relate to Richard Elmore's concept of the romanticizing of leaders?

4. In what ways might Monroe's description of what leaders do inform your practice or be worth sharing with colleagues?

STUDY GUIDE FOR CHAPTER 2: WORKING THROUGH CONFLICT

Thomas Sergiovanni wrote, "It's the leader's responsibility to be outraged when empowerment is abused and when purposes are ignored" (1992, p. 173).

1. Do you agree with Thomas Sergiovanni's statement that leaders have a responsibility to be outraged when empowerment is abused? Why or why not?

2. In Chapter 2, when and how did the principal express outrage, what do you think kept the principal from expressing outrage on other occasions, and what might she have done that would have been effective in addressing the outrage?

3. When have you expressed outrage or withheld outrage as a leader?

4. In what ways might Sergiovanni's comment about being outraged inform your practice or be worth sharing with colleagues?

Ronald Heifitz (2002) wrote, "The most difficult work of leadership involves learning to experience distress without numbing yourself" (p. 123).

1. Have you ever noticed numbing yourself the face of distressing events? If so, what did you do and what might you have done?

2. What can a principal do to guard against self-numbing during distressing experiences?

3. Do you think it would be possible for a principal to subscribe to Noddings's idea about leadership being an ethic of care and still resort to self-numbing during distressing situations? How so?

4. In what ways might Heifitz's idea about numbing inform your practice or be worth sharing with colleagues?

STUDY GUIDE FOR CHAPTER 3: COMMUNICATING WHO WE ARE AND WHAT WE BELIEVE

Peggy McIntosh (1985) wrote, "Many people, especially women, experience feelings of fraudulence when singled out for praise, press, publicity, or promotion. While such feelings of fraudulence may be deplorable, especially if and when they trouble women more than men, these same feelings also may indicate a wise reluctance to believe in the accuracy of absolute ranking and may point the way to a valid critique of hierarchical structures. . . . People who feel in public like imposters are perhaps more to be trusted than those who have never experienced feelings of fraudulence."

1. What are ways that the principal may have wondered whether she was a fraud and how might that have affected her leadership?

2. How do you think principals who are androgynous men or racial or ethnic minorities might react to McIntosh's concept of feeling like a fraud?

3. How do Richard Elmore's leader as hero and Peggy McIntosh's feeling like a fraud compare and contrast in relation to the principal's reflection on her practice?

4. In what ways might McIntosh's concept of feeling like a fraud inform your practice or be worth sharing with colleagues?

Daniel Goleman (1998, p. 190) wrote about the emotional intelligence of leaders, "A common failing of leaders, from supervisors to top executives, is the failure to be emphatically assertive when necessary. . . . Incompetence can show up in something as commonplace as failing to take the helm in a meeting and so letting it meander rather than steering it directly to key agenda items. Another deficiency in leadership in this area is the inability to be clear and firm. This results in workers not knowing what's expected of them."

1. How did the principal initially try to be assertive, and did she change her strategies during her career?

2. What have you observed staff do when principals are assertive? Are there ways you have seen principals be assertive that resulted in clarity without alienation?

3. How does this aspect of Daniel Goleman's concept of emotional intelligence relate to Peggy McIntosh's ideas about power and feeling like a fraud?

4. In what ways might Goleman's comment about assertiveness inform your practice or be worthy of sharing with colleagues?

STUDY GUIDE FOR CHAPTER 4: BUILDING COMMUNITY

Roland Barth (2006, p. 8) wrote,

> One incontrovertible finding emerges from my career spent working in and around schools: The nature of relationships among the adults within a school has a greater influence on the character and quality of that school and on student accomplishment than anything else. If the relationships between administrators and teachers are trusting, generous, helpful, and cooperative, then the relationships between teachers and students, between students and students, and between teachers and parents are likely to be trusting, generous, helpful, and cooperative. If, on the other hand, relationships between administrators and teachers are fearful, competitive, suspicious, and corrosive, then these qualities will disseminate throughout the school community.

Barth identifies four types of adult relationships: parallel play, adversarial, congenial, and collegial. He describes congenial relationships as being interactive, positive, personal, and friendly. Examples of collegial relationships are "educators talking with one another about practice, educators sharing their craft knowledge, educators observing one another while they are engaged in practice, and educators rooting for one another's successes" (p. 10).

1. How does the principal's growth over time relate to Barth's reflection about the importance of adult relationships and their impact on the school community?

2. What are some examples of congenial and collegial relationships in the principal's school, and how might the principal have facilitated moving the staff from congeniality to collegiality?

3. In any schools where you have worked, what was the relationship among the adults and does your experience support Barth's contention?

4. How does what Roland Barth wrote compare and contrast with Nel Noddings's ethic of caring and Ronald Heifitz's caution about self numbing?

5. In what ways might Barth's concept of congenial and collegial inform your practice or be worth sharing with colleagues?

Linda Lambert wrote that "Leadership . . . involves opportunities to surface and mediate perceptions, values, beliefs, information, and assumptions through continuing conversations; to inquire about and generate ideas together; to seek to reflect upon and make sense of work in the light of shared beliefs and new information and to create actions that grow out of these new understandings. Such is the core of leadership" (Glanz, 2006, p. 13).

1. In what ways, why, and how did the principal grow in the ability to surface and mediate perception, values, beliefs, information, and assumptions with the faculty and the students, and what were some missed opportunities to do so?

2. Have you observed the kind of leadership Lambert described, and if so, what was your reaction to it?

3. Do you see any connections between Linda Lambert's idea of generating ideas together and Peggy McIntosh's discomfort with a hierarchical system or ranking?

4. In what ways might Lambert's description of leadership inform your practice or be worth sharing with colleagues?

STUDY GUIDE FOR CHAPTER 5: ADVISERS, MENTORS, AND ALLIES

Meg Wheatley defines a leader as one who has more faith in people than they do in themselves and who courageously and patiently holds opportunities open long enough for their self-confidence to reemerge.

1. What are examples of when others had more faith in the principal than she had in herself and what was the effect on the principal?

2. How would you describe the principal's evolution as a leader in terms of Wheatley's definition of a leader?

3. What are some ways that the principal provided opportunities for staffs', parents', or students' self-confidence to reemerge, and what else might she have done?

4. Might Wheatley's definition of leadership inform your practice or be worth sharing with colleagues?

Andrew Young once described the Southern Christian Leadership Conference staff's reaction to three women portrayed by Marian Wright Edelman as "Great Black Women Mentors and Movement Builders" in this way: "We could deal with Septima [Clark] because she reminded us of our grandmothers. We could deal with Dorothy [Cotton] . . . because she reminded us of our sisters. But we could not deal with Ella Baker because she reminded us of our mothers. She held us accountable and tolerated no nonsense. None of us had come to grips yet with our mothers" (Edelman, 1999, p. 128).

1. Do you think the principal experienced some of the intolerance Andrew Young described because some staff responded to the principal as if she were the "mother" of the school? If so, how might the principal have dealt with this projection?

2. Have you ever observed leaders taking a parental role in their dealings with parents, students, or staff, and if so, what were the results?

3. How might Andrew Young's comment relate to Thomas Sergiovanni's belief about expressing outrage, and how do they both relate to the principalship?

4. In what ways might Andrew Young's insight inform your practice or be worth sharing with colleagues?

STUDY GUIDE FOR CHAPTER 6: REFLECTING ON A CAREER: COMMITTING TO PURSUE PROFESSIONAL PASSION

Stephen Covey wrote that "When you engage in work that taps your talent and fuels your passion—that rises out of a great need in the world that you feel drawn by conscience to meet—therein lies your voice, your calling, your soul's code" (Smith & Piele, p. 159).

1. Have you ever been in an environment where the leader reflected what Covey describes? How did that affect you and others around you?

2. Have you ever felt that passionately about your own work, and how did it affect you and others?

3. Do you see any connection between Nel Noddings's comments about an ethic of care and Stephen Covey's description of passion?

4. In what ways might Covey's description of work that taps your talent and passion inform your reflection on your career or be worth sharing with colleagues?

Marian Wright Edelman (1999) wrote *Twenty-five More Lessons for Life*, and Lesson 21 is "Be a good ancestor. Stand for something bigger than yourself. Add value to the Earth during your sojourn. . . . Every minute you drink from wells you did not dig, are sheltered by builders you will never know, are protected by police and soldiers and neighbors and caretakers whose names are in no record books, are tended by healing hands of every hue and heritage, and are fed and clothed by the labors of countless others" (pp. 166–167).

1. What value do you think the principal worked to add? What value did she try to add to the earth?

2. Can you identify giants on whose shoulders you stand? How have they, by their writing or their behaviors, affected your thinking about leadership?

3. As an educator and leader, what will be your legacy?

4. How does Marian Wright Edelman's lesson relate to each of the writers quoted in the study guides?

5. In what ways might Edelman's Lesson 21 inform your practice or be worth sharing with a colleague?

References

Barth, R. (2006, March). Improving relationships within the school-house. *Educational Leadership, 63*(6), 8–13.

Brooks, H., & Brooks, G. (1995). *Out of women's experience.* Thousand Oaks, CA: Corwin Press.

Covey, S. (2004). *The 8th habit: From effectiveness to greatness.* New York: Free Press.

Dunne, K. & Villani, S. (2007). *Mentoring new teachers through collaborative coaching: linking teacher and student learning.* San Francisco: WestEd.

Edelman, M. W. (1999). *Lanterns: A memoir of mentors.* Boston: Beacon Press.

Elmore, R. F. (2000). *Building a new structure for school leadership.* Washington, DC: Albert Shanker Institute.

Glanz, J. (2006). *What every principal should know about ethical and spiritual leadership.* Thousand Oaks, CA: Corwin Press.

Goleman, D. (1998). *Working with emotional intelligence.* New York: Bantam Books.

Hammonds, K. H. (1999, September). The Monroe doctrine. *Fast Company, 28,* 230. Retrieved December 24, 2007, from http://www.fastcompany.com/magazine/28/lmonroe.html

Heifitz, R. (2002). *Leadership on the line: Staying alive through the dangers of leading.* Cambridge, MA: Harvard Business School Press.

Lambert, L. (2003). *Leadership capacity for lasting school improvement.* Alexandria, VA: Association for Supervision and Curriculum Development.

McIntosh, P. (1985). Feeling like a fraud. Working Paper # 18. Wellesley, MA: Wellesley College Center for Research on Women.

Nieto, S. (2000). *Affirming diversity.* New York: Longman.

Noddings, N. (1992). *The challenge to care in schools: An alternative approach to education.* New York: Teachers College Press.

Rittenhouse, L. J. (Fall 2001). Leadership and the inner journey: An interview with Parker Palmer. *Leader to Leader, 22* , 26–33. Retrieved March 27, 2008 from http://media.wiley.com/assets/45/45/0787958026_Palmer.pdf

Sergiovanni, T. (1992). *Moral leadership: Getting to the heart of school improvement.* San Francisco: Jossey-Bass.

Sinetar, M. (1989). *Do what you love and the money will follow.* New York: Dell.

Smith, S. C., & Piele, S. C. (2006). *School leadership.* 4th ed. Thousand Oaks, CA: Corwin Press.

Villani, S. (2002). *Mentoring programs for new teachers: Models of induction and support.* Thousand Oaks, CA: Corwin Press.

Villani, S. (2006). *Mentoring and induction programs that support new principals.* Thousand Oaks, CA: Corwin Press.

Wheatley, M. (2001). *Leading in a networked world.* Burlington, MA: Linkage, Inc. Retrieved December 24, 2007, from http://ohcm.gsfc.nasa.gov/DevGuide/DevPrograms/LLseries/271.01%20Wheatley%20Part%20Mat.pdf

Williamson, M. (1992). *A return to love.* New York: HarperCollins.

Index

CORWIN
PRESS

The Corwin Press logo—a raven striding across an open book—represents the union of courage and learning. Corwin Press is committed to improving education for all learners by publishing books and other professional development resources for those serving the field of PreK–12 education. By providing practical, hands-on materials, Corwin Press continues to carry out the promise of its motto: **"Helping Educators Do Their Work Better."**